Children, Spirituality, Loss and Recovery

This book demonstrates the hopeful stance the young take in response to ordinary suffering and significant trauma when adults talk with them about their losses. Its underlying themes convey the truth that loss and recovery are normal in the process of growing to maturity. It examines the strength of the child's capacity for resilience through partnerships with adults who allow children to focus on the loss and tell the story of its meaning to someone who really hears it. The authors agree that adults need to perceive their own losses so that their attentiveness to the young is informed by wisdom that comes through self-understanding, but the authors also agree that many adults do not offer that help to children because they believe it will make matters worse.

Children, Spirituality, Loss and Recovery reveals this fear as a false notion by dealing with childhood traumas such as acquired disability, warfare, HIV/AIDS, death of one's parents and cultural dislocation. The authors are experienced practitioners who provide practical and theoretical insight into the dynamics of loss and recovery. This book offers hope for those who live and work with children and youths through its studied approach to addressing loss by describing young people's potential to work towards wholeness even in the face of fundamental losses to their security.

This book was previously published as a special issue of the *International Journal of Children's Spirituality*.

Joyce E. Bellous is Associate Professor of Lay Empowerment and Discipleship at McMaster Divinity College, McMaster University in Hamilton, Ontario where she has taught since 1993. She researches and teaches in the areas of spirituality, postmodernism, multiculturalism, culture, ethics and education. She is a consultant, speaker and writer for teachers, pastors, colleagues and congregants on the subjects of leadership and ministry education. Her special interest is children and spirituality.

Children, Spirituality, Loss and Recovery

Edited by Joyce E. Bellous

Routledge
Taylor & Francis Group

LONDON AND NEW YORK

First published 2010
by Routledge
2 Park Square, Milton Park, Abingdon, Oxon, OX14 4RN

Simultaneously published in the USA and Canada
by Routledge
270 Madison Avenue, New York, NY 10016

Routledge is an imprint of the Taylor & Francis Group, an informa business

Typeset in TimesNewRomanPS by Value Chain, India
Printed and bound in Great Britain by MPG Books Group, Bodmin, Cornwall

British Library Cataloguing in Publication Data
A catalogue record for this book is available from the British Library

ISBN10: 0-415-55136-6
ISBN13: 978-0-415-55136-6

CONTENTS

Notes on Contributors

Dr Carla Nelson has been an educator, counsellor, educational psychologist and administrator, for many years. In 1999, she was named the YWCA Woman of Distinction in Education for the city of Edmonton, Alberta. She has helped coordinate Canadian teachers to participate in programs of professional development for teachers in Kenya, Rwanda, Bolivia and India and continues to focus her research on teachers in transition.

Dr Jean Clinton is a child and adolescent psychiatrist at McMaster University in Hamilton, Ontario. She has worked in the mental health field with children and their families for over 20 years. She is a consultant to child welfare and mental health agencies in the Province of Ontario. Her research has turned to understanding the social determinants of health, particularly the crucial importance of the early years, and the importance of relationships in developing resilience. She is a fellow of Dr Fraser Mustard's Council for Early Child Development. As an advocate for children and youth she speaks throughout North America. Her greatest accomplishment and honour is being the mother of five great kids, ages 13–24 years.

Denise Peltomaki (MA) began ministry at Portico Community Church in Mississauga, Ontario, as Children's Pastor for 13 years. She was also on staff at Agincourt Pentecostal Church in Scarborough, Ontario. While at Portico, she developed and directed ministry strategies and programs for about 400 to 450 children. She is a consultant for educational practices that apply to children.

Rev Emile Sam-Peal has recently been appointed principal of the Lott Carey School, just outside Monrovia, Liberia. For 17 years he served as General Secretary of the Liberian Baptist Missionary and Educational Convention. Most of his tenure was concurrent with civil war raging in the country. Sam-Peal had to flee for his life with his family, as rebel forces advanced. He spent some time as a refugee outside of Liberia, but always returned in the hope of making a positive difference in his homeland. His strength of character is a model of resilience and recovery that others may note and emulate.

Professor Louise Rowling has been involved in research in the loss and grief field for over 25 years. Her research finding in schools that articulated the disenfranchised grief of teachers was the first acknowledgment globally, and her book, *Grief in school communities: effective support strategies* (2003) described a new orientation to loss and grief in schools. She is the president of Intercamhs, the International Alliance of Child and Adolescent Health, a member of the International Work Group on Death, Dying and Bereavement and of the editorial board of *Omega: The Journal of Death and Dying*.

Dr Elaine Champagne is an associate professor at the Institut de pastorale of the Dominican University College in Montreal, Quebec. She has worked for many years in paediatric pastoral care. Her researches focus on children's spirituality.

Dr Jane Bone lectures at the University of Auckland, New Zealand. She has been involved in early childhood education for a number of years. Her research interests include spirituality and well-being, alternative philosophical approaches to early childhood pedagogies, and ethical issues when conducting research with young children.

Dr David A. Walters (PhD, CSci, FHEA) is currently a college professor of Psychology at Keyano College, Fort McMurray, Quebec, as well as a research associate in the Department of Psychology, University of Chester, UK. He has worked as a psychotherapist and clinical psychologist both in Canada and the United Kingdom. Dr Walters' current research interests include existential and humanistic models of counselling and psychotherapy, as well as the application of existential principles to pedagogy and learning in higher education.

David Erickson (PhD, RPsych) holds a research associate position at the Glenrose Rehabilitation Hospital in Edmonton, Alberta, and is also an associate clinical professor of Paediatrics in the Faculty of Medicine and Dentistry, University of Alberta. He is a licensed psychologist and has counselled with children for many years.

Abstracts

We are all affected: considering the recovery of HIV/AIDS infected and affected children
Carla Nelson

This chapter acknowledges that the HIV/AIDS pandemic has created entire communities for whom loss has become a common and a shared experience. As a result of this impact of HIV/AIDS, several questions surface. However, the one question upon which this chapter focuses is, 'What type of environment is required for children infected and affected by HIV/AIDS?' More specifically, 'What context can be created by educators and concerned adults for children infected and affected by HIV/AIDS in order to help them recover a glimmer of wholeness and sense of connection again?' Drawing on eight years of involvement with educator colleagues in several African countries, the chapter suggests one avenue through which recovery can be encouraged: by giving attention to the environment which teachers and other concerned adults can provide. Such an environment must work against ignorance, stigma and isolation.

Resilience and recovery
Jean Clinton

The theme for this chapter identifies a shift in psychological, psychoanalytic concern from an individualistic interpretation of human experience to one that offers a systemic approach to a child's life. Resilience research departs from previous patterns in which psychological insight was grounded on what we knew about individuals in terms of their present and past experience. In describing resilience as a systemic approach, this chapter examines responses children make to trauma and loss, by looking at a whole world experience that shapes and informs those responses. Resilience research identifies external factors and internal characteristics of those children that develop their capacity to thrive under stressful conditions and recover after they have *experienced loss.*

The purpose of the chapter is to show that, by understanding the capacities some children have for resilience, others might gain knowledge to continue more meaningful lives despite, or perhaps due to, a significant loss. In addition, that knowledge may inform and inspire the adults who care for them. The possibility of recovering from loss is a human potential: as Confucius said, 'Our greatest glory is not in never falling, but in rising every time we fall'. Using several case studies, the author outlines the nature of resilience and picks out its role in recovery to make the point that resilience, i.e., doing well, despite adversity is an outcome of a set of interrelated components in a child's life. The argument is made that resilience relies for its development on relationships among positive personal responses to crises, a caring family, and a civil community.

An afflicted waiting
Denise A. Peltomaki

This chapter demonstrates that affliction is a state of anguish that has physical, social and psychological dimensions as well as spiritual ramifications. In this way, affliction is the most profound form of suffering, as it leaves no area of life unscathed. The chapter – written from a confessional perspective – explores the following concepts in the greatest detail: the agony and activity of waiting for the sufferer, the persistence of hope, and the longing for spiritual transformation through affliction. With respect to loss and recovery in children, it is becoming increasingly evident that adults must become comfortable in talking about loss and recovery in their own lives; they must communicate their own stories of anguish so that they can better hear – and respond to – what children communicate about their own losses. Therefore, the author's own journey through affliction (resulting from a motor vehicle accident), is described in the latter half of the chapter.

Pastor Emile's children
Emile Desmond Ebun Sam-Peal

This chapter outlines the efforts of one man in a war-ravaged country to make a radical difference in the lives of children that have suffered the consequences of civil strife. The author was leader of a Baptist denomination in Liberia throughout a period of a civil war that devastated the country. Despite personal and political turmoil, he is an example of someone that cares deeply for children. He continues to act on their behalf so they may imagine a better future. His primary approach in helping Liberian children to rise from social chaos was to speak with them about their ultimate concerns and spend his time listening to their responses. The purpose of the chapter is to recommend his simple process and to suggest that listening to children tell their stories and share their dreams is a constructive and meaningful interaction in which their value as persons is perceived and affirmed, an action that is particularly significant to those that have experienced the fundamental losses inherent in civil warfare, in which many children were forced to fight themselves.

Linking spirituality, school communities, grief and well-being
Louise Rowling

This chapter proposes that school communities are significant public places that help shape identity and can also contribute to social and emotional well-being. If school communities respond appropriately to crises and trauma that affect the young, learning becomes social and emotional as well as academic. School communities offer an opportunity for positive impact, since, during times of crisis – as they are experiencing loss and grief – children and youth turn to parents, peers and teachers to help them make sense of their worlds.

Several aspects of making sense of the world are implied in this chapter, namely, finding a sense of meaning and purpose, experiencing coherence in relation to life goals and feeling a degree of connectedness towards school and schooling. These aspects influence well-being in children and youth. An argument is made to promote whole school communities by exploring the kind of community schools can become when they attend to spirituality as a sense of connectedness and if they address loss and grief holistically. In outlining qualities of a whole school community approach, linkages are made among terms such as spirituality, loss, grief and mental health to reveal the importance of people and place in the well-being of children and adolescents. The chapter proposes that creating a whole school community approach relies on acknowledging a communal experience, not only the individual experiences, of loss.

Living and dying: a window on (Christian) children's spirituality
Elaine Champagne

Faith and beliefs about living and dying are fundamental constituents of spiritual development. However, children are seldom asked to talk about their experiences of life and death. This chapter has a twofold purpose. It first describes children's expressions on living and dying, as heard during a newly developed programme which encourages children's participation as active subjects of their spiritual journey. This programme, the Grande Halte, began in 2004 within the changing context of Christian religious education in a secular Québec. Secondly, it proposed a theological reflection informed by the social sciences and the social context of the milieu, and based on children's expressions. It suggests that stories and symbols are needed in order to develop a coherent horizon of meaning in one's life. The relational dimension of the process is also highlighted.

Exploring trauma, loss and healing: spirituality, *Te Whāriki* and early childhood education
Jane Bone

Attention to spirituality is proposed to be a means of restoring and supporting well-being in early childhood educational contexts. In Aotearoa, New Zealand, the spiritual dimension is included in the early childhood curriculum *Te Whāriki*. This holistic approach to education supported research in three different early childhood settings: a Montessori *casa*, a private preschool and a Rudolf Steiner kindergarten. Narratives (re)produced from the qualitative case study data are included in the chapter to show that young children experience and overcome adversity in their early years. The discussion is framed by the cultural theories of everyday life and attention to philosophical perspectives that encompass the spiritual. Spiritual withness, spiritual in-betweenness and the spiritual elsewhere are introduced as spiritual and transformative spaces in these settings. This account combines research, theory and pedagogical perspectives. It describes the concept of everyday spirituality as an ameliorating factor in these stories of loss and recovery.

Grief and loss: towards an existential phenomenology of child spirituality
David A. Walters

Western cultures have taken on a death-denying and grief-avoiding dimension, suggesting that children in particular are to be protected from the harshness of loss and death. As a result, many children grow up without having consciously experienced the pain of major loss and grief. It is argued that having been spared from suffering, from the pain of working through their grief, they are being subjected to a form of emotional and spiritual abandonment by those around them. As Søren Kierkegaard asserts, it is these very adults who come to play the role of 'thieves' or 'bandits' in their misguided attempts to protect children. As father of existentialism, Kierkegaard and his followers have suggested notions of self, being and spirit that assist in developing a phenomenology of child spirituality.

The existential understanding of *spiritedness* or *spiritual directedness* appears particularly suitable to children, given their innate qualities of openness, the desire to understand, their qualities of innocence and purity. The case of Simon is discussed, not only his adjustment to major loss, but movement through various *modes of being* that require self-assessment, dialectical relationship, and the active choice required of existential psychotherapy. As such, it is argued that when a child is assisted in making grief meaningful, he or she is also afforded an opportunity to enrich their spiritual resourcefulness and that this serves as both model and inspiration to adults around them.

Spirituality, loss and recovery in children with disabilities
David V. Erickson

This chapter focuses on loss, recovery and spiritual dimensions of trauma in spinal cord injury (SCI) during adolescence. From a clinical perspective, while there are physical characteristics in common with congenital childhood disabilities such as spina bifida, life adjustment issues associated with acquired disabilities can be quite different, and may have lower reported life satisfaction. There is little information about adolescents who have experienced SCI and the role of spirituality in the rehabilitation process. To explore that relationship further, this article uses a case study approach of a 15-year-old female adolescent who had acquired a SCI in a motor vehicle accident that claimed the lives of her mother and grandparents. Her story was gathered through several interviews and was examined in terms of her spiritual perspectives. The purpose is to present implications, informed by other adolescents as well, that help family, health-care providers and other adults, especially teachers, to understand her needs.

Introduction

This book offers diverse views on human spirituality but has strong themes in common. At the heart of every author's concern for children and youth is a belief that the spiritual needs of the young call for particular responses from an adult world – a world they depend on for the sustenance that comes through the security of their sense of connection to it. During trauma and disruption, feeling meaningfully linked to other people, oneself, and Something Beyond ordinary humanity, lights the pathway to recovery and signifies the possibility for effectively incorporating loss into a project of becoming more mature as a human being, one that is able to feel hope for oneself and the world.

This book generally agrees that the adult world, for many children and youth, often fails to provide them with sufficient resources to meet their spiritual need for a satisfying sense of connection, and in response, they offer remedies for the sense of disconnection that many children and youth may experience. Providing useful practical approaches as well as relevant theory is the purpose of this book.

In addition to acknowledging the need for connection, authors agree that we should begin to respond to the young by listening to their stories, told in their own words, which include their own perceptions of their grief and what recovery might look like for them. In each chapter, children and youth are perceived as active, fully engaged participants as they struggle to understand and move through the periods of grief that accompany significant losses. The stories embedded in this work are testimonies to the strength and insight that children and youth already have about their experience; yet, while many children and youth are portrayed as remarkably resilient, these articles remind us of their vulnerability, a condition of youth that adults must take seriously. As this book points out, perhaps the most prevalent belief of many adults is that they should not speak about loss in the presence of those who suffer, because it may somehow make a child or young person feel worse about their situation. This could not be farther from the truth. The young want to be heard: listening to them and telling them our stories of loss and recovery are salient ways to express spiritual connectedness.

What is it that makes us all so vulnerable to the need for connection expressed by the children and youth whose stories are told in this book? How is it even possible for a bounded psycho-physical unit – the human person – to experience connection to self, others, God or Something Ultimate? I suggest that a need for connection is universal because every infant endures the same loss. At birth, we are cut from our mothers when the umbilical cord is severed. After that, we learn to breathe on our own. Human spirituality is an accommodation inherent in our nature to address the breach of that first connection. From birth, we are not released as isolated, solitary beings: living on our own is not the same as feeling lonely. It takes time for children to become self-sufficient. That lengthy apprenticeship is meant to persuade the young that the final aim of human maturity is interdependence, not independence. That metaphysical umbilical cord, once severed at birth, has an end that must be joined up somewhere, or to someone. Otherwise the sense of felt connection withers and may atrophy. Maturity is encouraged through the healthy attachments that we enjoy, while outcomes of a shrivelled sense of felt connection are expressed in depression, suicide, addiction and endless striving for significance that has a way of perpetually evading its pursuers.

For everyone, loss and recovery play a pivotal role in becoming healthy in, through, and sometimes in spite of, ordinary human attachments. A human need for attachment is inescapable. Sadly, these attachments may wither, or be unwelcome. They may be sources of suffering and radical disappointment. But attachments also can be sustaining, healthy links to inter-subjective experience. I think it is a task of human wisdom to learn where and with whom the healthiest connections are found and made. At its roots, human spirituality is a natural and supernatural reality (Bellous 2006). I make this claim, not to privilege one religious view over others, but rather to say that people, due to the ways we become human, inevitably have some notion that there is *Something There*. In asserting that the spiritual has natural and supernatural dimensions, I do not want to eliminate the secular from the discussion. Rather, I want to say that, whether one is secular or religious, young people need from us a large enough picture of the world so they can find and make a home for themselves within it. Secular traditions must provide a big picture for the young, as do religious traditions.

Using a second metaphor, the human spirit is an agent of communication that permits us to connect and reconnect with others and remain in touch with ourselves. It is an active agent that constructs meaning in the form of concepts we have of ourselves, others, the world, God (even if it is unfavourable) and our ultimate concerns. I define spirituality as a sense of felt connection to say that people are able to read the world, and must learn to do so effectively in order to make sense of experience. That world is more than material reality. It is also relational; spirituality is formed and sustained through relationship. Children and youth need opportunities to speak about what really matters to them without feeling judged for their point of view, so they can reflect on the quality and kind of connections they are seeking. As they take these opportunities, the human spirit actively makes meaning, relying on emotional and social intelligence to do so (Goleman 2006). Meaning-making is a funda-mental activity of the human spirit.

Robert Kegan (1982; 1997)[1] focused attention on meaning-making activity by re-examining Piaget's stages of development to point, not to the plateaus Piaget identified, but to the process of meaning-making whereby a person moves from one plateau to another. To Kegan, during meaning-making activity, a normal flow of human development is character-ised by continuous events of loss and recovery. As an example, from infancy, cognitive capabilities of human beings grow and develop as a subject, an infant, is embedded in object experience and then dis-embeds herself from those objects. The 'movement involves what Piaget calls "decentration," the loss of an old center' (Kegan 1982, 31). For example, a newborn does not distinguish himself from his mother until evidence emerges through separation anxiety that he understands that his mother is distinct from him and can be lost. An infant perceives she can be lost and experiences a threat to his connection to her. As another example, infants are unaware they possess reflexes through which they interact with the world – they are embedded in the subjectivity of these reflexes. Yet around two years of age, they begin to perceive these reflexes and gradually move from being the subject of them to having the self as an object of their own perceptions. Now that they are dis-embedded from their reflexes, they can think and reflect on them.

Such a process of differentiation, however, does not result in a new object; reflexes are not now outside the self and the loss does not complete the transformative process. It is not until a process of 're-centration', or integration, occurs that developmental transformation can move forward. Upon emerging from that to which one was subject, the new object must be recovered and internalised in order for the child to relate to it. That is, for a young child to truly reflect on their reflexes, they must internalise them as a recovered object on which they can reflect. In so doing, '[t]he move from being my action-sensations to having them creates a new subjectivity. In "having them" they are integrated into a more articulated psychologic' (Kegan 1982, 31).

Kegan's analysis, briefly outlined above, of decentration and recentration, differentiation and integration, loss and recovery, conveys what people continue to do throughout the whole of life. These processes are fundamental to humanity. All learning requires that loss and recovery become a normal part of one's meaning-making activity. Kegan's theory implies that adults are wrong to think children and adolescents are unable to deal with loss, even significant, traumatic, overwhelming loss. Facing and recovering from loss are part of what ordinary infants have been doing since birth, is a normal function of meaning-making. The young have a capacity to address loss and recover from it, but they need true companions in order to do so in a healthy way.

Spiritual health is a consequence of feeling connected to the world and people in it, feeling contentment with God (whatever one's view is), and/or feeling satisfied with the particular ultimate concerns that focus and direct our lives. Spiritual processes create meaning about the world, loosely systematised into the worldviews that we organise from personal experience.

A worldview is a way of thinking about the world, ourselves, others, God and ultimate concerns. It is a relatively stable system by early adolescence. Meaning systems or worldviews are tested over a lifetime by subsequent experience. Worldviews may shift or resist change; the actual connections we make can be formative, informative and transformative during that process. Over time we are compelled to look for people, places, ideas, sometimes substances that allow us to feel well connected. During the process of these revisions, children and youth may become able to revisit their worldviews in order to weave their losses into the fabric of their lives. With self-reflection, the self becomes aware of itself, which Hegel depicted as self-consciousness of self-consciousness; he used the term experiencing to capture this activity (Heidegger 1989).

To ground its natural, self-reflective dimension as a meaning-making activity, I came to define spirituality as a sense of felt connection by examining five ordinary human processes, namely cultural, neurological, sociological, biological and psychological processes (Bellous 2006). But that was before I read the research of Eugene Gendlin (1962, 1981). He offered philosophical and psychological dimensions of what he called a 'felt sense' or 'experiencing', as he put it. His notion added to insights Hegel explored in his concept of experiencing and educator Paulo Freire (1993) described as *conscientiasation*, which refers to *being with* one's own thinking.

Gendlin outlined the psychological dimensions of a felt sense in addition to its philosophical and educational roots. To him, a felt sense is a large, vague apprehension, layered with thought and emotion that is more than a feeling. It unites mind, heart and body in awareness that profoundly influences one's life because it has been shaped by personal experience. It is an embodied, internal sense encompassing everything a person 'knows' about a subject, situation or problem. A felt sense tends to communicate itself all at once, with all its complexity, rather than giving the detail by detail account of what we are experiencing. A felt sense is like an experience of tasting something you can't quite put words to, or a sense one has in listening to music by giving full attention to it. It is not simply thinking; it is not just a feeling. It is both. It has a powerful impact: it is 'a big round unclear experience' (Gendlin 1981, 22). If the body is like a computer, so experience is stored on a hard drive and is available to us if we give it our full attention.

Gendlin began researching a felt sense by analysing thousands of patient and doctor interviews. He was able to identify in advance the people who would benefit from treatment and those who would not likely benefit. He made his predictions by noticing a competency that some clients had from the start to engage in what he called focusing: a type of paying attention in which they got access to the felt sense they had about the specific problems they brought to the psychologist or psychiatrist. If I had read Gendlin prior to defining human spirituality, I might rather have called spirituality *a felt sense of connection*. I think a felt sense is like the 'oceanic feeling' that one of his friends tried to convey to Sigmund Freud (1955) in response to Freud's rejection of religious experience.

Learning from experiencing loss, and recovering from it, is an opportunity to gain wisdom that accrues by paying attention to the effects of particular objects to which we attach ourselves and their effects on the worldview continually being formed, informed, and transformed within us. The relationship between people and objects of attachment selected over a lifetime shapes the worldview, values and expectations we develop. That relationship is powerful in directing how people view the world and manage themselves within it. Listening well to someone who is describing the felt sense they have about a loss is also powerful in its capacity to help people sense more fully the complexity of what they experience – its suffering as well as its opportunity (Bellous and Sheffield 2007, 55–7).

Earlier I suggested that human spirituality and its healthy development depend on social literacy. Social literacy refers to the developed capacities involved in our encounters with others and our own authentic responses during those encounters that move social interaction toward positive outcomes based on mutual respect and caring (Goleman 2006, 84). As we listen to a felt sense of one who is grieving, our capacity for social investment, and their capacity to comprehend their grief, is enhanced. I make this point because another theme that ties together this book on loss and recovery has to do with a belief that we have a fundamental responsibility for one another, particularly for those who suffer loss, even when they live in countries we have never visited. Social literacy, based on social intelligence, is a capacity to value other human beings; it is a universal demand. Let me first describe social literacy before I make an argument for its global application.

Social literacy is based on social intelligence, i.e. a range of capacities from instantaneously sensing another's inner state to understanding someone else's feelings and thoughts; it implies an ability to comprehend complicated social situations. Goleman (2006) divided social intelligence into two sets of attributes under the terms *social awareness* and *social facility*. The first category, social awareness, is a capacity for feeling with others and sensing nonverbal emotional signals. It relies on attunement or listening with full attention and receptivity to another person. It also includes empathetic accuracy, i.e. understanding another's thoughts, feelings and intentions in a way that the other person would affirm as accurate. Social cognition knows how the social world works. All four aspects of social awareness are homework for learning social literacy.

The second set of attributes is called social facility by Goleman. They refer to an ability to sense how others feel, so that we 'know' what they think or intend and can adapt to their needs during an interaction with them. Skill in social facility does not guarantee that social interactions will be positive, but it does mean we can learn from social interaction rather than simply letting it happen to us. Social facility teaches us over time to create smoother, more effective interactions. It does so as we pay attention to synchrony (acting and interacting smoothly and nonverbally) and offering an effective, intentional self-presentation (the ability to influence and shape the outcome of social interactions). Facility also requires that we care for another's needs so we both listen to them and act accordingly; in so doing, we demonstrate that we heard have them. It is not sufficient to listen to others; we show that we have heard them by acting on knowledge gained through social interaction. Awareness and facility are dimensions of social intelligence that enable people to learn to be socially literate.

While Goleman does not use the term, I suggest that social literacy refers to competence in social intelligence, which Goleman thinks can be learned. Being competent is not the only goal for those who would be socially literate. Learning to be socially literate provides people with other civil competencies. A developed capacity for social literacy grounds secular and religious views so that people become cosmopolitan in a sense spelled out by moral theorist Kwame Anthony Appiah. To him,

> Each person you know about and can affect is someone to whom you have responsibilities: to say this is just to affirm the very idea of morality. The challenge, then, is to take minds and hearts formed over long millennia of living in local troops and equip them with ideas and institutions that will allow us to live together as the global tribe we have become. (2006, xiii)

The cosmopolitanism Appiah promotes is distinguished from multiculturalism and globalisation and has at its centre two interwoven strands of thought: one is that we have obligations to others that stretch beyond kith, kin and citizenship; the second is that a sense of obligation is not meant to neutralise the significance of particular people's values, beliefs and ways of life that are close to us (xv).

Cosmopolitanism, as he stipulates the term, is a challenge to address our need to live well with local and global realities. What obligates us toward each other is a thread of humanity that unites the human tribe, an idea with a long tradition. That earth's citizens are connected is congruent with Immanuel Kant's moral framework. He thought 'obligation applies to all of us since the earth is round and connected. As a consequence, every part of the earth affects other parts and people cannot escape these effects without leaving the face of the earth' (Gregor 1996, 50). To ground moral obligation, Kant made a model for humanity focused on male heads of households. Using gender exclusive language, he said mankind has a duty to himself on the basis of the humanity within him *as a sensible being* and *as a free being*. In so saying, he formed an idea for modern humanity.

Kant constructed moral obligation on the bases of duties to oneself and to God's existence. Along with the assignment of duties, one could expect to enjoy certain rights. To Kant, obligation was communal and personal. We have a personal duty to ourselves to act in accord with the value of humanity that is within us. Our duty to ourselves is just like the duty we have to others. While Kant did not say it this way, he was aware of the privilege we attach to our own perspective. We know ourselves better than we know anyone else, although less well than we like to think (Gregor 1996, 155). For the most part, we make sense to ourselves and know what would make us happy. Other people are less easy to grasp. It is only recently, then, that rights were applied to humanity itself, rather than being the specific privileges attached to duties.

With a proliferation of rights, came an increase of obligations in the form of social duties, so to speak, but they can also be linked to the general development of human rights over the last several decades. As British social theorist Edward Miliband observed,

> the eighteenth century saw individuals granted civil rights (equality before the law), the nineteenth and early twentieth century brought political rights (equality of the franchise), and the early twentieth century onwards, [encouraged] social rights (based on principles of equal access to education, health care, housing [as some examples]. (2005, 40)

Miliband is not naive in describing human progress. He refers to developments in human rights as a rough and ready assessment of that period of history.

In addition to advancements Miliband outlined and during their development, Marx recognised a need for humanity's material support. He saw that 'the senses of human being can operate at a merely animal level – if they are not cultivated by appropriate education, by leisure for play and self-expression, by valuable associations with others', and American philosopher Martha Nussbaum (2000) added freedom of worship to his list (73). Marx supported Kant in prizing humanity but departed from Kant by 'stressing (with Aristotle) that the major powers of a human being need material support and cannot be what they are without it' (Nussbaum 2000, 73). Nussbaum's analysis of human needs adds a further dimension, by implication at least, though it is not specifically stated by her.

If Marx argued persuasively for humanity's material resources, Nussbaum's work implies a fundamental human need for relational resources so that all people may live a truly human life. She is not alone in her assertion that we cannot live truly human lives if we are caught in social conditions of relational poverty, but her philosophical analysis is persuasive and clear. It is not only a desire to ameliorate effects of racism and sexism that drives her demands for relational support. In many schools in North America, children suffer physical and emotional bullying – a telltale sign of an absence of adequate, equal relational support for those caught by abuse. In the current development of rights language, the centrality of healthy relationships is understood to play a pivotal role. It is more essential to have healthy relationships and receive adequate attention from our environment than it is to have lots of money. Relational support is felt primarily in adequate, appropriate attention from one's environment; just as we can see who has wealth, social power and value, discerning those with an ability to get and keep attention is a marker of plenty in terms of human worth and social privilege (Derber 2000).

This book, focused on loss and recovery, assumes as a fundamental condition of existence that we need each other and owe each other adequate relational support. Part of that support requires that adults reflect on their own stories of loss and recovery so they can be good listeners to children and youth in their care; therefore, included among these articles is one story of extreme suffering, an afflicted waiting, told by a young woman. The aim of its inclusion is to practice what we preach about telling our stories so that we can understand loss empathetically. Other articles assert that children and youth, since they are inherently spiritual meaning-makers by virtue of being human, are capable, strong and resilient but need adult support. Our aim is to provide theoretical and practical insight into loss and recovery in order to help us all be better companions to children and youth – those who experience ordinary existential loss as well as those who experience traumatic loss. Our purpose is to show that loss and recovery shape the meaning we make of the world. To face loss hopefully is a contribution we make to each other and to the next generation's capacity to be healthy and whole adults.

Note
1.   I am indebted to David Csinos for some of the analysis of Robert Kegan's theory in these paragraphs.

References

Appiah, K. 2006. *Cosmopolitanism: Ethics in a world of strangers.* New York: W.W. Norton.
Bellous, J.E. 2006. *Educating faith.* Toronto: Clements.
Bellous, J.E., and D. Sheffield. 2007. *Conversations that change us.* Toronto: Clements.
Derber, C. 2000. *The Pursuit of attention.* Oxford: Oxford University Press.
Freire, P. 1993. *Pedagogy of the oppressed.* New York: Continuum.
Freud, S. 1955. *Civilization and its discontents.* London: The Hogarth Press.

Gendlin, E. 1962. Experiencing and the creation of meaning. New York: The Free Press.
———. 1981. *Focusing.* New York: Bantam.
Goleman, D. 2006. *Social intelligence* New York, Bantam.
Gregor, M., ed. 1996. *Kant: The metaphysics of morals.* Cambridge: Cambridge University Press.
Heidegger, M. 1989. *Hegel's concept of experience.* San Francisco: Harper & Row.
Kegan, P. 1982. *The evolving self.* Cambridge, MA: Harvard University Press.
———. 1997. *In over our heads.* Cambridge, MA: Harvard University Press.
Miliband, E. 2005. *Does inequality matter?* In *The New Egalitarianism,* ed. A. Giddens and P. Diamond, 39–51. Cambridge: Polity.
Nussbaum, M. 2000. *Women and human development* Cambridge, Cambridge University Press.

Joyce E. Bellous

We are all affected: considering the recovery of HIV/AIDS infected and affected children

Carla Nelson

Introduction

There is a phrase that I continually hear when I am in Kenya, a phrase that speaks of the prevalence of HIV/AIDS. It is chorused by children and adults, students and teachers, faithful and non-faithful, rich and poor, unemployed and politicians, shoeshine boys and businessmen. It is the phrase, everyone is either 'infected or affected'.

I am not used to hearing such phrases. On my Canadian landscape of school classrooms, student services offices, and teacher preparation discussion tables, I have never knowingly encountered HIV/AIDS directly. I have been involved in conversations on school policy that have instructed schools on the importance, even imperativeness, of using gloves when dealing with an injured, bleeding student. I have been a part of health lessons which have investigated communicable diseases and the protective strategies to implement to prevent them. I have even been a part of student service clubs that have raised funds for AIDS orphans and other vulnerable children. Yet in each of these cases, I have entered in with layers of protection keeping me from personally being 'infected or affected'. But when the opportunity came for me, a teacher from the prairies of western Canada, to participate in a series of professional development initiatives with Kenyan teachers in their home country, I sensed that these protective layers would be penetrated. They were, and I too became, affected.

My purpose in dedicating this essay to the impact of loss and recovery on the spiritual lives of children is to explore the profundity of the phrase, 'everyone is either infected or affected'. In brief, the phrase exposes the reality that the HIV/AIDS pandemic has created entire communities for whom loss has become a common and a shared experience. While many questions surface, the one upon which my reflection has focused over the past eight years of collegiality with teachers in various African countries is the question as to what type of environment is required for children infected and affected by HIV/AIDS. What context can educators and concerned adults create for children infected and affected by HIV/AIDS to possibly help them recover a glimmer of wholeness and sense of connection?

Global impact

Although they can be difficult to understand, HIV/AIDS statistics demonstrate the overwhelming devastation the disease has had in our world. The UNAIDS office in Geneva provides the following overview of the disease's impact (UN n.d.) and I attempt to offer a graspable comparison. To demonstrate the extreme damage that HIV/AIDS has had on the world, I will compare some African statistics to the population of my home country of Canada.

- 25 million people have died from HIV/AIDS in the past 26 years. The entire population of Canada is approximately 33 million (Statistics Canada n.d.).
- In 2006, 3 million people succumbed to the disease. In the same year, there were 3.9 million children between the ages of 5 and 14 in Canada (Statistics Canada n.d.).
- Also in 2006, an estimated 4.3 million people were newly infected, which means that there are more new infections than there were AIDS related deaths (UN n.d.). Of these, young people (15–24 years of age) accounted for 40% of these new infections. It is not surprising, then, that experts say that the course of the world's HIV epidemic hinges in many respects on the behaviours that young people adopt or maintain, and the contextual factors that affect those choices.
- The most striking increases of contraction have occurred in East and Central Asia and Eastern Europe.
- Each day, today, 6500 Africans will die from AIDS.
- Each day, today, 1500 children become infected with HIV, the vast majority of whom are newborns.
- In sub-Saharan Africa, approximately 9% of children under the age of 15 have lost at least one parent to AIDS and one in six households with children is caring for at least one orphan.
- 40 million people are currently living with the disease.

What kind of environment do children infected and affected by HIV/AIDS need in order to dare to hope for some kind of recovery? They need to experience one in which there is some kind of wholeness. After many conversations with Kenyan educators and church leaders, I, along with many others, suggest that children affected and infected by HIV/AIDS need a just environment. They need an environment in which their questions can be heard and answered, in which knowledge about the disease is accessible, and in which they themselves – regardless of their own HIV status and their family's reputation with the disease – are accepted. This type of context will require their adult world, whether it is in school classrooms or in faith communities, to bring an end to three specific injustices: ignorance, stigma and isolation.

End the ignorance

Ending ignorance requires access to information. One helpful definition of poverty is that it is a lack of access: it may be a lack of access to clean water, food, a sustainable income, financial credit, affordable health care, an education or to many of the basic necessities of life. The poverty of access to education has far reaching affects. Children therefore need access to education, especially if ignorance about HIV/AIDS is to cease.

Whenever I have had the opportunity to ask children whose lives have been, or are being, directly affected by AIDS, what they hope for most, their answers inevitably include the unmitigated dream of being able to attend school. I am continually taken aback by this response because I live in an environment in which parents and teachers are constantly cajoling their children to get up for school in the morning, to get their homework done, and to take advantage of the myriad of opportunities that await them.

But children infected and affected with HIV/AIDS believe that school represents hope and that education facilitates recovery. I once asked the children at my faith community in Toronto what they thought the kids in Africa hoped for most. After their responses, which ranged from relative astuteness (such as saying that African children want love, homes and Jesus), to relative inanity (such as pizza and iPods), their usual chorus of hand-waving turned to absolute silence when they finally realised with horror that African children just want to be able go to school.

The reasons as to why 18% of the children in the world do not attend school range from those that can be easily understood to those that, as Stephen Lewis so aptly states, defy logic in a civilized society (Lewis 2005). At the comprehensible end of the continuum, reasons include having to stay home to nurse an ill parent or having to work at whatever income-generating activity the child can access, be it selling vegetables or selling themselves, in order to compensate for an ill or absent parent. I once witnessed children generating a meager income by sorting through a garbage dump for cigarette butts. They adeptly gathered each strand of unburned tobacco into dirty plastic grocery bags which they in turn sold back to the tobacco company. In India, I met children who thought they were the lucky ones because they were paid by the gravel company to use their nimble agility to climb the quarry walls, in their bare feet no less, to strategically place dynamite. Interestingly, the career counselling program I instituted at the high school in Canada where I used to teach did not include either of these two career options in their myriad of future job opportunities.

Here are two examples of reasons which, to me, are at the incomprehensible end of the continuum. First, many children do not have access to school because there are no teachers to instruct them. At certain times of the pandemic in Africa, more teachers have died of AIDS than have graduated from teachers' colleges. In Kenya specifically, a report published in an October 2002 newspaper stated that 18 registered teachers die every month. This shortage became vividly clear to me as I was visiting some colleagues in northern Angola. As we drove into their village, I commented to them that I was thrilled to see two classrooms bursting full of children in the school we were passing. My excitement immediately dissolved when they responded, 'The children have been waiting for three days for a teacher to show up'. Because the teachers had not been paid for eight months, one teacher was forced to drive a taxi just to make a bit of money for the necessities of his household. The school had not been able to locate the other. She was feared dead.

Second, children do not have access to school because they can not pay the fees which, unbelievably, were initially instituted in many African countries because of international policy. Stephen Lewis, the former UN special envoy to Africa, traces this injustice to the structural adjustment policies of the eighties and nineties. These policies, he says, did extraordinary damage to the African economy, from which they have yet to recover. They were policies based on conditions: loans were secured only if certain conditions were met. Lewis does not mince words on this topic.

The conditions ranged from the sale of public sector corporations, to the imposition of 'cost-sharing' (the euphemism for user fees imposed on health and education), to savage cut-backs in employment levels in the public service, mostly in the social sectors. To this day, the cut-backs haunt Africa: the IFIS (international financial institutions) continue to impose 'macro-economic' limits on the numbers of people (think nurses and teachers) who can be hired, and if that doesn't do the trick there are financial limits placed on the amount of money that can be spent on the social sectors as a percentage of the country's gross national product. The damage is dreadful. One of the critical reasons for Africa's inability to respond adequately to the pandemic can be explained by user fees in health care (people can't afford to pay for treatment) and user fees in education (that is, school fees) which helps explain why so many orphans are out of school. (2005, 5)

Lewis goes on to state that

virtually the entire onus should be on the World Bank and IMF [International Monetary Fund] to cough up the money that governments and individual schools lose when the abolition of fees is introduced. After all, the concept of 'shared costs' or the equivalent euphemism, 'user fees', lies at the root of the destructive fee policy and those responsible for the ideological destruction *Weltanschauung* should also be responsible for its reversal. (2005, 169)

Such destructive ideologies have far-reaching humanitarian implications. They allow 'world economic problems to be taken out on the growing minds and bodies of young children is the antithesis of all civilized behaviour. Nothing can justify it. And it shames and diminishes us all' (Lewis 2005, 25).

Some African countries, including Kenya, have already boldly abolished school fees. In January 2003, just days before the new school term, the then new president of Kenya, President Kibaki, finally declared that education in the country is to be compulsory and free to Standard 8. The first Monday morning of the new term, it is estimated that 1.2 million more children showed up to register for school than had been registered in the previous term. Several of my Kenyan colleagues told me that the populations of their schools increased by one third. Suddenly, they had 19 year olds in their grade-1 classes. They reasoned that if you have never been to school, you need to start at the beginning. One mother brought her daughter to school for Standard-1, and she, the mother, joined the Standard-2 class. A newspaper published the picture of an 81-year-old man, dressed in uniformed short trousers, as he entered into his very first class at school.

These colleagues of mine reflect on those first days of 'free' schooling as being some of the most joyful days in their teaching careers. They were absolutely overwhelmed by the chaos it created, but they were also absolutely overjoyed at the thought that every child in Kenya was now welcome in school. There was never a day they were more proud to be teachers.

This was a bold beginning, but, as every parent knows, schooling contains many other costs: books, uniforms, and fees for parent-teacher associations, community associations, and examinations. What is required is universal, unimpeded, unequivocal free education with absolutely no costs, hidden or otherwise. Again, as Lewis reminds us, 'That's what it says in the Convention of the Rights of the Child; that's what the international community, in theory at least, has agreed to' (2005, 91).

The research is substantive and all of it supports the fact that primary education is the salvation of struggling societies. It demonstrates that every additional year of schooling, beyond providing the glorious wellspring of knowledge, brings with it the best chance to defeat poverty and better parenting, health, and nutrition. It also provides greater opportunity and a direct line to economic growth (Lewis 2005, 95).

The UNAIDS office draws a clear conclusion: 'Evidence from Uganda shows that a child who does not go to school is three times more likely to be HIV-positive in his or her twenties than a child who completes basic education' (UN n.d.). To be protected from having to incur additional loss and in order to have the tools for recovery, children need to be in school with teachers who have themselves been given access to education about the disease. From this statement, it is clear that teachers themselves need access to education.

One person who is providing teachers with such education is Mrs Martha Nthenge, one of my heroes. She is in her mid-sixties, has a nursing background, and is now a trained counselor for HIV/AIDS-infected and -affected women in Nairobi. She accepted the invitation to lead an HIV/AIDS training day for teachers in her home district of Machakos, Kenya.

Her introductory comment as the day began was not a litany of her accomplishments or her credentials or family pedigree. It was not even a prayer or a devotional reading. It was a welcome: 'May all of you feel welcome here. Especially those of you who are HIV-positive, may this place be a place of welcome'. At one point in the day, while addressing matters of intimate sexuality, Martha reached into her bag and pulled out a small package containing a female condom. She opened it and ensured that every one of her 40 Kenyan colleagues and five Canadian friends held the lubricated tube-like anathema. This was a first for the vast majority of us in the room; we were all confronted with the realisation that we cannot teach that which we do not know.

Kasimbi was in the training session that day. He peppered Maratha with questions, many that most Kenyan men, even professional men, would not have dared asked in such a forum. He was especially confounded by a section in the textbook in which the high risk of HIV contagion during the birth process was discussed. His questions would not have been given a voice if not for a group of high-school students from Regina, Saskatchewan, Canada. These young people sold enough hot dogs and book marks to raise sufficient funds to purchase 40 comprehensive and up-to-date HIV/AIDS textbooks written by a professor in South Africa. Each of the teachers in the seminar received one of these textbooks. A colleague reported to me that Kasimbi, this experienced teacher of 16 years, called the 33 midwives who worked in his community to a seminar to give these women access to this information. Teenagers from the prairies of Canada helped teachers in Kenya to stave off unnecessary experiences of loss.

Martha's inclusive training day generated a confidence among that group of 40 teachers. The day had indeed offered them an experience of belonging, a place of welcome, and a space of safety. They knew that they needed to replicate that type of learning environment in each of their classrooms. They decided that together, they would create a manual of lessons addressing aspects of HIV/AIDS. Since their experience with Martha had provided them a safe place in which to discuss the details of the content that they needed to first learn, they wanted to articulate how safe classroom environments were established, to determine which pedagogical strategies would best facilitate learning, and to identify the assessment mechanisms by which they would know the children were learning. After 18 months of writing, piloting, editing and re-piloting, they had printed a collection of 40 lessons as a teacher resource to accompany the national AIDS syllabus. To date, two thousand copies of the manual have been printed and distributed. Teachers throughout Kenya have been in-serviced by the cohort of 40 teachers as to how to use the manual. And, the manual has even served as a basis for a cohort of teachers in Indonesia to create their own manual relevant to their context. All this was possible because Kenyan teachers and Canadian students realised that, in order to end the ignorance about HIV/AIDS, they needed to see that they are all affected.

The critical need to end ignorance is the hope that every classroom will be a place where accurate information is provided, where questions can be asked, and where a caring community of learners – teachers and peers together – can be nurtured.

End the stigmatisation

I knew that stigma was still an issue, even amongst our extremely caring and accepting gathering of teachers outside of Nairobi, when Beatrice, one of the teachers, put out a plea to the class for blood donors. Beatrice's 15-year-old son required emergency surgery. The doctor estimated that she would need 10 pints of blood to be available to her during the procedure. Although the blood bank would provide her with these pints, it is the responsibility of the family to replace the required amount of blood. So people muster up friends and family to assist. However, in a land where HIV infection is so prevalent, it is difficult to find 10 uninfected persons. Beatrice presented the situation to the class.

The class chairman, Muthengi, then did something that I thought was odd. Instead of asking for a show of hands right there and then, an action that would be considered perfectly acceptable where I come from, Muthengi requested that those who wished to, and were able to, donate their blood ought to speak to him in private after the session. It dawned on me that Muthengi did not want to put any teacher into the position of having to say that he or she was not able to donate because of being HIV positive. It made me wonder, if we, a group of supposedly professional and enlightened educators who have the benefit of not living side by side in neighbourly proximity, have not created a safe enough environment, how difficult it must be for a community based group, like a local congregation or a school, to offer an environment of acceptance.

But this is what is required. Ending stigma is the mandate to make every place a safe place in which to declare my HIV status, to receive a warm and caring welcome, as a student or a teacher, and to know that this place is one in which I can speak out about my HIV status and my levels of affectedness.

Why can't people make such declarations of their status as HIV-positive? Although there are many reasons, let me present two for consideration. First, it may be because we are better at being judgmental than at being compassionate. Second, it may be because HIV/AIDS is largely a female concern.

Women are at the forefront of those affected by stigma of HIV/AIDS, which is increasingly being called a 'woman's' disease. Sociology will attest to the fact that any 'thing', be it a disease or a profession or a cause, that is mostly associated with women gets less attention from the rest of the world. Breast cancer is typically less funded than prostate cancer. The decline of the respectability of the teaching and even the psychological professions can be correlated with the rise in the number of females who participate. So is the case with HIV/AIDS.

Women experience the impact of HIV more severely than do men. Two excerpts from the United Nations AIDS organisation offer more insight into the connections between gender and AIDS:

> The effects of gender inequality leave them more at risk of exposure to HIV. Less access to education and economic opportunity results in women being more dependent on men in their relationships, and many who have no means of support must resort to bartering or selling sex to support themselves and their children. Where women can't own property and lack legal protection, their dependence within their families is even greater. Women and girls are also at increased risk for HIV infection biologically. In unprotected heterosexual intercourse women are twice as likely as men to acquire HIV from an infected partner. (UN n.d.)

[Women] assume the bulk of care giving when their male partners, children, and parents fall ill. Women with HIV and women whose partners die of AIDS often suffer discrimination and abandonment. In a study researched in India, almost 90% of the HIV positive women inter-viewed were infected by their husbands, but the women were often blamed for their husbands' illnesses. (UN n.d.)

The fact that there are courageous examples to the contrary offers hope to this injustice. Many churches and schools in Kenya, Rwanda and Angola have coordinated what they call Guardians of Hope cooperative groups.

'Guardians' is their name for themselves. They see themselves as the vanguards, the safeguards, the ones called to care for those infected and affected by AIDS. These guardians have made the courageous choice to welcome orphans into their homes and to become the parent. Often, they are a relative of the ones they welcome. Many of the guardians are grandparents, grandmothers in particular, who have no means of income and yet absolutely believe that the best place for a child is in a home.

I visited one Guardians group at a church on the outskirts of Kigali. Pastor Jonas knew that he had to do something radical to minister to his congregation of which the majority of members are HIV positive.

I imagine many pastors worldwide would have great difficulty in welcoming those who have AIDS into their midst. They would struggle with health risks and budgets. Building a community around HIV positive people will likely not help fulfil any long-range strategic plans nor raise revenue. But for Pastor Jonas, the health risk to himself, his family members and his other parishioners is less than the risk of watching at arm's length as your commu-nity literally dies away.

For Pastor Jonas, his vision is to have a community which is known for finding ways to help the parent or grandparent buy the required uniform for each child. In the case of one woman I met, aptly named Faith, it was a school uniform for each of her own eight children plus one for each of the five children now in her care since the death of her sibling.

This community uses small sums of money as loans for a few members to start a busi-ness, maybe hair styling or vegetable selling. They help families find yet another place to stay. So many of them have been asked to leave their rented rooms when the landlord has found out that their disease may leave them unable to pay the rent, or may make it difficult for the landlord to rent the room again if it becomes known that an AIDS sufferer died there, or may leave the landlord with a mess to clean up later. For so many, it is just simply easier and more rational to not get involved.

Pastor Jonas set, as one of the requirements for membership in this community, the mandate to produce the paper on which the clinic stated the member's positive HIV status. In other words, he reversed the stigma. Rather than hiding it, the members needed to declare it to themselves, their families, and their community. This courageous step sets the stage for inclusion and belonging.

Stephen Lewis predicts that 'Eradicating stigma will be the last holdout in the epic battle against AIDS' (2005, 69). But this difficult task is essential in understanding HIV/AIDS and helping others to overcome it. One important way to end the stigmatisation is to create class-room environments wherein infected and affected children will feel no need to hide the pain of their loss and no shame for their circumstances. After all, we are all affected.

End the isolation

I wish to tell you a bit more about Pastor Jonas' community in Kigali. Seventy adults, mostly women and, as I stated earlier, all HIV positive, had each miraculously saved and willingly paid the 1000 Rwandan francs (about two US dollars) necessary to join the cooperative. After realising that the church could be the place in which they find belonging, Pastor Jonas convinced them that the first step towards helping themselves was to help one another.

The members of this community do not want much – not any more than most of us want: food for their kids, schooling for their kids, a place to live for their kids, some hope for their kids. They also want a fund they can use to buy a small gift to take when they visit their bed-ridden members. Might a Bible be too much to ask for? And what about the possibility of being able to purchase a coffin so that when healing comes through death, it and their friend can be given the dignity both deserve.

Each Thursday when they meet as a cooperative, every adult contributes another 50 Rwandan francs – only ten cents, but enough to buy eggs for a meal, perhaps enough for a day's rent, a fortune that is freely given to one of their own who needs it most. It is there, through the giving, that they find joy. It is through sharing their weakness that they are made strong. It is through sacrificing all, that they are finding life. It is through admitting their loss that recovery can begin.

A community in Mitaboni, Kenya, has also instituted a Guardians of Hope cooperative. With the gratitude and pride that comes with a bumper crop, several members of this group gave me a tour of their glorious garden. The head teacher is the agricultural mastermind behind this glimpse of Eden. Sweet potatoes, tomatoes, beans, corn, onions, *sakuma-weki*, carrots and potatoes were oozing out the ground before me. Every family in the group was getting all the food they needed, and, with the extra, they were supplementing their incomes and the group's savings by selling the surplus at the local market.

I asked about the children and the orphans of the area. They told me that, in addition to the orphans who were now living in their own homes, there were several child-headed households – households who had no adults left alive – living as neighbours to several of them. For these child-headed households, the cooperative gives food from the garden and even tithes 30% of the supplemental income from produce sales to pay for the school fees and other expenses of these households. Without this assistance, the children would be dispersed, likely to orphanages. The tragedy of a move to an orphanage, the group explained to me, is that the children will lose the only collateral they have – their little homestead. Someone else would surely move onto the land in the children's absence and call it their own. The children would have no hope in ever getting it back. This community is making recovery possible. This is reason to celebrate.

Conclusion

What type of environment is required for children infected and affected by HIV/AIDS? What context can be created by educators and concerned adults for children infected and affected by HIV/AIDS to possibly help them recover a glimmer of wholeness and sense of connection again? To facilitate recovery, children infected and affected by HIV/AIDS need an environment in which they will find belonging, in which they will not be stigmatised because of their circumstance, and in which their losses will be acknowledged. Every classroom can be such a place.

References

Lewis, S. 2005. *Race against time*. Toronto: Anansi.
Statistics Canada. n.d. Statistics. http://www.statcan.ca (accessed December 10, 2007).
United Nations. n.d. General information. http://www.unaids.org (accessed December 10, 2007).

Resilience and recovery

Jean Clinton

Introduction: two case studies

One scenario: Two girls woke up to another morning of shouting between their parents who were arguing about their older brother because he had not come home again the previous night. Each parent was working at two jobs, trying to climb their way out of the poverty of an inner city subsidised housing project. Anna, scowled, as she put on the same clothes she wore yesterday, and she worried about what the kids at school would say about her. The other, Jenna, was already thinking of an art project her teacher assigned. She did not notice her mismatched socks as she waltzed into the kitchen, seeming almost oblivious to the tension that was thick in the room.

Another scenario: Two boys, John and Ryan, dozed in the back seat after an intense weekend at a basketball tournament when suddenly the van spun out of control and crashed into the side of the road. Three of their team mates were killed in the accident, but John and Ryan, sitting together at the back, were miraculously unhurt – or so it seemed at the outset. Both went back to school to resume their routine, but altered life. Counsellors were available to all students, but neither of these two boys went to see them. After several months John still woke up with night-mares, his grades were dropping, he seemed to have lost interest in many of his favourite things, and he refused to talk about the accident. His parents, initially concerned, were increasingly frustrated that he wasn't 'getting over it'. Ryan, though initially very sad and frequently emotional, appeared to be back on track. He spoke of their lost friends and wanted to start a basketball scholarship in their names, which was a surprise to those who knew him since before the accident, he was seen as quite shy and retiring.

Why is it that these children, similar in some characteristics, when faced with risk and trauma, have such different psychological outcomes? Why is it that for some young people, challenge leads to growth and change, yet for others only to more suffering? Questions such as these led researchers in the 1970s to explore an observation that some children develop well under risk conditions, while others do not. These researchers believed that understanding the factors and conditions that led to better outcomes in some children and youth could improve the life chances of all children who encounter hazardous experiences (Masten and Obradovic 2006, 14), such as those that were affecting Anna, Jenna, Ryan and John.

In this article, I explore the concept of resilience and propose that it is not a personality or inborn trait as was once thought; rather, resilience is a manifestation of a complex interaction of factors, both genetic and environmental. To make this point, I examine resilience as a form of adaptive behaviour and then apply its theory to the case studies above. Following that application, I will discuss the interactive relationships between a child's biology and his or her environmental conditions to show that neither biology nor environment alone can account for resilience. I will conclude with suggestions to show how the principles gained from resilience research can be applied to individual children and youth in the family and in society. Implicit in the discussion is a belief that children and youth can handle crises better if protective factors, skills and conditions are intentionally fostered in the family and in the community that surrounds it.

A new way of thinking about adaptive behaviour

Resilience refers to doing well, despite adversity. Its research points out that the behaviour associated with the term is not simply part of someone's personality; it is not something some people are born with and others are not born with. It is a type of adaptive behaviour, a set of observable traits that arise when someone is faced with the difficult scenarios that Anna, Jenna, John and Ryan were experiencing. The term refers to an ability to rise above adversity and come out the better for it. People who demonstrate resilience are those who thrive in the face of trouble. Two of the children in the scenarios described above are able to adapt to difficulty in positive ways; two are not so able. How are we to understand the adaptability that Jenna and Ryan are expressing?

Adaptive behaviour in general, which can be defined as the ability to cope with the demands of one's environment, includes self-help strategies, communication and social skills. Adaptive behaviour has for a long time fascinated researchers, clinicians and parents alike. Until the 1970s, the study of typical human development and the study of abnormalities in psychological development (psychopathology) were predominantly two separate disciplines. The merging of these two perspectives led to the field of developmental psychopathology. As these two discourses were linked, resilience research benefited from their marriage because, as a form of adaptive behaviour, resilience requires that someone *both* be exposed to an adverse event or conditions *and* demonstrate an outcome in which that person does better than would have been expected. For example Jenna and Ryan's exposure to risk was similar to Anna and John's but the outcomes differed. What is it about Jenna and Ryan, and their interaction with the system within which they lived, that led to differing outcomes, i.e. to their positive pattern of recovery?

As scientists examined the descriptors, underlying processes and conditions that led to positive responses in young people such as Jenna and Ryan, the field of resilience research unfolded. The exploration was greatly influenced by Bronfenbrenner's ecological systems theory, which held as a core idea 'that human individuals are living systems continually interacting with the contexts in which their lives are unfolding, including family, peer groups, schools and larger systems' (Bronfenbrenner 1979).

The pre-eminent scholar and child psychiatrist Sir Michael Rutter also posits that resilience research started by recognising the huge individual variation in people's responses to the same risk experiences. As an example, some children who lived with parents who had schizophrenia did not fare well, while their siblings did. Rutter suggested that if we could understand 'the mechanisms underlying that variation [it would] cast light on the causal processes and, by so doing, [would] have implications for the intervention strategies with respect to both prevention and treatment' (Rutter 2006, 43) of children and youth undergoing significant stress.

In contrast to the systemic approach associated with resilience studies, previous research looked at external circumstances and examined their effects on individuals. As examples, researchers asked about the effects on a developing child of environmental conditions such as poverty, single parenthood, dangerous neighbourhoods and parental schizophrenia. In contrast, the idea of resilience moves from focusing on external risk to investigating how external risks are dealt with by an individual relying on his or her dynamic internal processes. In one way, resilience researchers turned their field glasses around and looked through the other end: they focused not on the far object, i.e. the environment in which a child struggled, but looked close-up at internal processes of the child, the object near to hand. They studied children who were experiencing loss, rather than only examining the environment that necessitated their adaptive behaviour.

For example, Anna and Jenna were exposed to the same conditions of external risk: both experienced living in poverty, they shared the same parents, whose educational attainment did not improve during the girls early years. Yet they responded differently. What are the factors that led to their different adaptations? Is a healthier response an outcome of birth order, temperament, differences in their exposure to abuse, their intelligence, having preferred status in an important arena, or, is it simply that one of the girls got better genes for adaptive behaviour? Jenna's behaviour constitutes a better way of adapting to her situation, since she accepted mismatched socks and didn't worry what people would say about her. Her behaviour is a positive adaptation because she was able to think about an art project she looked forward to as a way of expressing her talent.

It is important to clarify that *resilience* is a term used in many contexts and is easily confused with other concepts, such as competence, coping, positive mental health, or even resiliency. Coping and adapting describe behaviour that is a response to stress; these strategies do not imply that the behaviour is positive or successful. We can be coping with stressors by simply going through the motions of our day-to-day rituals, as one example. Resilience refers to behaviour that is a constructive, positive adaptation to stressful situations.

Resilience is also different from resiliency. The latter term is a characteristic, or ability, to return to a previous level of functioning after a stressful experience; some would say it is a better descriptor of rubber bands than it is of people. Resilience, on the basis of my first-hand knowledge as a psychiatrist, as well as on the research, refers to being transformed and altered by an experience of adversity so that one is not the same: the person with resilience does not return to a former state of functioning, but is actually better off. Resilience describes individuals who do not simply cope, but recover in a way that demonstrates they are moving on with life in a thoroughly positive way.

The characteristics of resilience

Individuals such as Mother Teresa, Pope Jean Paul II, Bill Clinton or Oprah Winfrey, to name some exemplars, are people who have faced significant adversity and demonstrated resilience. They had difficult early life experiences and not only overcame adversity but became great in at least some capacity. In the past, we may have thought they were invulnerable, superhuman, somehow inoculated against the conditions of their childhood. Such thinking was reflected in the 1970s by articles like one in the *Washington Post*, March 1976, which stated, 'Trouble: A bubble to these kids', a headline implying that some children could simply burst the bubble of adversity around them and move on. This view of children and adversity was followed by the myth of the 'golden child', one who stood in the midst of despair, yet remained gleaming and unscathed. The problem with this view of childhood and youth was that it promoted an idea not only that the resilient children were somehow special but also that resilience was a quality given only to a few.

These attitudes to recovery intimate that somehow children who bounce back from difficulty have been untouched or unaffected by those experiences or that they have superhuman traits that make them invulnerable to difficulty. As a result, people tended to think that resilience was an inherent quality of an individual – some people have it, some people do not. This is not only a false construct, but it minimises the effort and success of young people who have overcome adversity. The Latin term for invulnerable means 'not to wound' and intimates that one is incapable of being hurt or that one is immune to attack. It is essential to understand that resilient people have been attacked, felt the wound, were affected by adverse events, but they have surmounted them. What is it about them that allowed them not only to survive but to thrive? The answer may come as a surprise, since it lies in what they are able to rally to their aid.

Resilience does not come from rare and special qualities, but from the 'everyday magic' (Masten 2001) of ordinary, normative human resources in the minds, brains and bodies of children, as well as in their families, relationships and communities. The ongoing study of resilience has revealed that the adaptive behaviour connected to it arises from interactions within and between individual organisms (human beings) and their environment. As Masten discovered, what began as a quest to understand the extraordinary revealed the power of ordinary experience. The characteristics of resilience, then, are ordinary capacities people have internally (within the child) and externally (within the family and the community).

Characteristics within the child

Masten's work was informed by a longitudinal study, Project Competence, which followed 205 children and families from the 1970s to the present. The study continues with over 90% of its initial population still participating (more than 20 years later). As she looked back over the data collected on these children, she observed that young adults that demonstrated resilience in their twenties had shown the following characteristics in childhood, namely

- Good intellectual and attention skills
- Agreeable personality in childhood
- Achievement motivation and conscientiousness

- Lower stress reactivity
- Parenting quality in childhood and adolescence
- Positive self-concept
- Competence in childhood conduct, academic and social.

Some might think that these characteristics are inborn, but in fact most are manifestations of interaction between biology and the environment. For example, the development of attention skill requires attentive care-giving in infancy and nurturing, warm responsiveness when setting limits in toddlerhood. We learn to inhibit our impulsiveness and focus our attention as we are embraced by our family members and at schools. A positive self-concept comes from the experience of doing well and being acknowledged for that accomplishment. Children who are bombarded with messages of what they are constantly doing wrong develop self-concepts that are negative and self-defeating. So what is it about Jenna that makes her resilient?

On the surface, we could read her story and decide that she just doesn't get it – that she is not paying attention to what is going on in her household, that her sister actually has a better grip on reality. However, according to resilience research, Jenna has a different outlook, one of optimism. She appears to have a more agreeable personality. Is that because she is temperamentally less intense, so she can let things go and is thereby easier to parent and subsequently receives less negative attention? She has lower stress reactivity; things don't stress her as much as they do her sister. When events are stressful, she is able to get back to a pre-stress state more quickly. We all know people who can't let go of issues and get stuck and even make themselves sick. The ability to leave issues aside requires the self-reflective ability to say, 'I can deal with this later'. This response is developed through having positive experiences of successfully dealing with challenges.

Anna, by contrast, is stuck in a negative outlook. She has not been able to see beyond the moment that is 'stressing her out'. Perhaps as the older of the two girls, she has had more responsibility placed on her shoulders, which has left her feeling resentful. Perhaps she has a temperament that dislikes change, is slow to warm up, gives out less warmth in social inter-action so that her family members feel less secure in her love for them. She may be prickly in new situations; due to the overriding stress of poverty, her parents may be unable to find a way to help her identify her negative emotions and to mature by reflecting upon them.

Jenna has a sense of purpose and can focus her attention on her interests and exclude distracters. She is aware of the conditions in her family, she focuses on what can be, rather than on what is absent in her environment. Perhaps she epitomises the African proverb, 'It is not what you call me, but what I answer to that names me'. Anna, however, can think only of what she does not have.

But resilience is more than optimism. Jenna has faced the difficulties and has continued in an intentional way to be hopeful. It is not that she is oblivious to her circumstances – something else is going on. Masten concluded that she and her colleagues

> learned that youth who overcome childhood adversity and continue on to adult success have more protections and resources in their lives than their peers who do not fare as well. We observed 'late bloomers' whose lives took a dramatic turn for the better in the transition to adulthood, suggesting that new resources, opportunities, and supports converge in this window to promote positive change. (Masten 2008)

Another group of researchers under the direction of Harvard university professor Stuart Hauser and colleagues addressed the processes that underlie resilience. They interviewed 67 teens who had been significantly enough disturbed as teenagers to be admitted to a locked unit in a psychiatric facility. Their book, *Out of the woods* (2006) tells the stories of four of these youth who have not only survived but are thriving. Sadly, only nine of the 67 young people were doing well at all; many continued to lead very troubled lives. By looking at their narratives from the time of their admission to the facility at age 15 until adulthood, Hauser's group could delineate three characteristics crucial to resilience:

- Personal agency and a concern to overcome adversity
- A self-reflective style
- A commitment to relationships (Hauser et al. 2006, 39).

In Hauser et al.'s terms, Jenna and Ryan had a sense of agency – a sense that what they do matters and that they could intervene successfully in their lives. They believed they could make a difference even when their optimism was challenged. Rather than be emotionally beaten by the loss of his friends, Ryan wanted to make meaning out of their deaths by creating a scholarship in their names. He had a sense that he could make a difference. He may very well have had a family that understood that his reticence stemmed from introversion, not avoidance; they may successfully have communicated that they accepted him as he was and were available to provide support when he asked for it. In contrast, John's behaviour suggests that he was feeling isolated and lost. He did not use others as a means of comfort or seek out assistance. This reaction is seen often in children whose parents cannot meet their emotional needs when they are upset, distressed or ill. Attachment theory proposes that when children have predictable adults in their life that respond to their emotional needs, they will face stressors (stress-inducing events) better. If caregivers avoid responding when children need them, or are unpredictable in their responsiveness, the young develop a working model or worldview that tells them people are not reliable. This can lead them to give up and focus the blame for their difficulties outside of themselves, rather than looking for ways to be agents of change.

   Masten and Hauser et al. discovered that competence and developmental tasks at one age are effective forecasters of good future development; that is, resilience tends to endure. Yet they also learned that late resilience is possible: many thriving young people did not demonstrate resilience as they struggled through earlier hardships, but they did so eventually. This is a profound lesson and brings parents, teachers and counsellors much hope, although resilience research also points out that the child or young person has to express receptivity to that positive affirmation and support. Resilient children are those that can tell the story of their lives; that is, they are reflective of their experience; they can stand back from their difficulty and hence impact the story in positive ways.

The characteristics within the family

A crucial factor appeared in the lives of children who showed resilience: it was the presence of a secure base, a safe harbour. Children and youth who demonstrate resilience had one or more adults who loved and believed in them and remained connected to them in order to provide consistent emotional support. Grandparents, uncles, aunts, friends and teachers had shone the magic of connectedness on these children and encouraged resilience in their lives. Models of family functioning described by Olson, Russell and Sprenkle (1989) identify three characteristics central to healthy families, which are

- Cohesion, which facilitates togetherness
- Adaptability, which balances flexibility and stability
- Clear, open, consistent communication.

Research studies demonstrate that healthy families solve problems with cooperation, creative brainstorming, and openness to others (Reiss 1980), which is a point of research that is very similar to the processes described by Hauser. If families feel they can make a difference in a difficult situation and exert positive control over some aspects of it, better outcomes ensue. In addition, having the ability to reach out to others for support appears to be a characteristic of resilience, both in individuals and in families. This reaching out includes maintaining ties to institutions and social groups. Schuster and others found that 90% of Americans surveyed immediately after the 9–11 attacks reported turning to prayer, religion or spirituality in an effort to cope (Schuster et al. 2001).

Resilience is a construct, a theory that identifies the cumulative effects of a way of functioning that has positive outcomes when people face trouble with the attitude that 'this too will pass'. In terms of family dynamics, resilient families are less reactive; they employ creative brainstorming when difficulty arises and they express openness to others.

The characteristics within the neighbourhood

The well-being of the family is also impacted by the neighbourhood. In the community at large, resilience is strengthened when there is cohesion among neighbours, adaptability and open and consistent communication. Dr Felton Earls is the lead researcher in a multi-year, multimillion dollar study called the Project on Human Development in Chicago Neighborhoods. He is studying the impact of neighbourhoods in Chicago on development. He co-authored a pivotal paper in 1997 appearing in *Science*, in which the authors proposed 'that the differential ability of neighborhoods to realise the common values of residents and maintain effective social controls is a major source of neighborhood variation in violence' (Sampson et al. 1997, 918). They hoped that the notion they termed 'collective efficacy' would become a buzzword among social scientists and policymakers. Collective efficacy is a form of social cohesion among neighbours, in which they understand that they are all willing to intervene on behalf of the common good (918). At the heart of the concept is 'Trust, reciprocity, and a willingness among people to look out for one another', and Earls also notes that 'cities that sow community gardens may reap a harvest not only of kale and tomatoes, but safer neighbourhoods and healthier children' (cited in Hurley 2004).

Froma Walsh, from the University of Chicago, also studied traumatic loss and gave a compelling argument for expanding the focus from individual symptom-focused intervention to an approach that 'taps strengths and resources in relational networks to foster healing and posttraumatic growth' (Walsh 2007, 2007). As with individuals and families, when a neighbourhood believes in its collective efficacy in resolving its own difficulties, it acts out the characteristics that inhere in resilience.

Biology and environment

The topic of resilience also requires that we address the role of genetics. There is a continuing debate in the literature about whether a 'resilience gene' exists. One of the most exciting areas of research currently is the study of *epigenetics.* Genetics is the study of DNA-based inherited characteristics in organisms; epigenetics looks at factors that affect gene *functioning*, without changing the actual DNA. Imagine the workings of a computer in which DNA or the genome (the complete set of 23 chromosomes) is the hardware; epigenetics is the software that tells the genome how and when to work, as well as how hard to work. Others liken it to a metaphor using words and stories: the DNA is the words, but the story is ever-changing through the frequency and timing of particular words, and this is the epigenome. Epigenetics is a branch of research concerned with gene and environment (G×E) interactions and is the next great frontier in science.

As part of this early epigenetic research, the Dunedin study is a large longitudinal study from New Zealand that is providing ground-breaking evidence of genetic and environmental interaction. Researchers know that people are born with variations in their genes depending on their parents' contribution. We get one set of genes from each parent. A gene often comes in two varieties (such as a gene for eye colour that makes eyes brown or blue). An individual can thus have two copies of the gene of the same variety (brown-brown or blue-blue), or two copies of different variety (brown-blue). When looking at serotonin, a neurotransmitter in the brain known to be involved in depression, researchers found that people receive serotonin transporter genes from their parents that have either two short alleles (like the blue-blue above), two long alleles (like brown-brown), or one long and one short allele (blue-brown).

There is a relationship between the length of alleles and a tendency toward depression, but what the researchers discovered is that unlike eye colour, in which these genes cause eye colour, the mere presence of these alleles is not enough to *cause* depression. Rather, in people who have both the presence of two short alleles (making them vulnerable to depression) those who also experience maltreatment in childhood experienced high levels of depression (Caspi et al. 2003). Similarly, with the gene that regulates another neurotransmitter, monoamine oxidase inhibitor A, which is seen to be low in people with antisocial or conduct problems, low levels alone do not lead to difficulty; but if children have low levels of these transmitters and they also experience maltreatment in childhood, their problems soar (Caspi et al. 2002). Rutter also concluded that findings like these strengthen the idea that there is not a single universally applicable resilience trait. From the perspective of biology and environment, resilience is an outcome of the interaction of genetic makeup and environmental effects, which is also why, when neighbourhoods act together and believe that their collective actions can have significant effects on their quality of life, they are thought of as resilient.

Conclusion

Resilience research offers hope to children and youth as well as to their parents, teachers and counsellors. But how does research help parents, teachers and community members to foster resilience in the young? The evidence in the research suggests that what matters is a basic sense of connectedness with others through attachment and social support. The oft used African proverb, 'It takes a village to raise a child', truly is the heart of resilience; but we need also to recognise that sometimes 'it takes a child to raise a village'. Children can be exemplars of resilience and can teach us how to recover from loss in a way that makes all of us more human. If parents are supported in their attempts to be emotionally responsive and available to their children and focus on the development of social relatedness with them and other community members, they will enhance the role of empathy throughout childhood and into young adulthood.

This develops the pathways for empathy and resilience to work together. Too often parents are challenged to focus their attention on making children behave well, rather than emphasising a desire that they should grow up to be people that can love well. If we accomplish the goal, a second factor comes along with it. Children become able to regulate emotion, arousal and behaviour. If they are given opportunities to learn and experience effectiveness, they develop what is called self-efficacy, which is having a sense that 'I can do it'. Self-efficacy is a fundamental attitude in civil life if and when it is paired with a child who knows how to be open to and to love others. Civic-mindedness, then, is having a sense that what you do matters.

The four young people in the opening scenarios can now be viewed through the lens of resilience. They have access to varying levels of internal strength in terms of attention, ability to regulate their emotions, ability to relate to others, and hope for the future. Does this mean that Anna and John are doomed? Not at all. What resilience research tells us is that they are demonstrating a greater need for supportive environments, for people in their lives who can help them construct a new narrative, a new meaningful story around which to live their lives. People can come around Anna and John, people who can focus on what they do well, who believe in them and who will help them develop internal strengths and the capabilities to cope, develop competence and hope.

Hope is perhaps the greatest internal characteristic of resilience. In addition to having hope, we need to learn how to ask for help. Humour is important to resilience as an adaptive response. As well, 'viewing ourselves and others in terms of strengths not weaknesses; and having some kind of meaning in life – which does not necessarily mean having a formal religion', but it does mean having a large enough story to live in that we can feel at home in the world. 'Ultimately, a sense of connectedness lies at the heart of resilience'(Deveson 2004, 3). As Ghandi said, and showed us, as human beings, our greatness lies not so much in being able to remake the world – that is the myth of the atomic age – as it is in being able to remake ourselves.

Acknowledgements
The author would like to thank the many families who have shared their stories and taught her the magnificence of the human spirit and the courage to heal in the face of trauma and loss. Without the support of her own loving family her eyes, ears and heart would never have been open for the telling.

References
Bronfenbrenner, U. 1979. *The ecology of human development: experiments by nature and design.* Cambridge, MA: Harvard University Press.
Caspi, A., J. McClay, T.E. Moffitt, J. Mill, J. Martin, I.W. Craig, A. Taylor, and R. Poulton. 2002. Role of genotype in the cycle of violence in maltreated children. *Science* 297: 851–4.
Caspi, A., K. Sugden, T.E. Moffitt, A. Taylor, I.W. Craig, H. Harrington, J. McClay et al. 2003. Influence of life stress on depression: moderation by a polymorphism in the 5-HTT gene. *Science* 301: 386–9.
Deveson, A. 2004. The importance of 'resilience' in helping people cope with adversity. *Australia's e-journal of social and political debate*, http://www.onlineopinion.com.au/view.asp?article=1847
Hauser, S.T., J.P. Allen, and E. Golden. 2006. *Out of the woods: tales of resilient teens.* Cambridge: Harvard University Press.

Hurley, D. 2004. Scientist at work – Felton Earls: on crime as a science (a neighbor at a time). *New York Times,* 6 January.

Masten, A.S. 2001. Ordinary magic: resilience processes in development. *American Psychologist* 56: 227–38.

———. 2006. Developmental psychopathology: pathways to the future. *International Journal of Behavioral Development* 30, no. 1: 47–54.

———. 2008. Competence, risk, and resilience in development. http://cehd.umn.edu/icd/faculty/Masten.html

Masten, A.S., and J. Obradovic. 2006. Competence and resilience in development. *Annals of the New York Academy of Sciences* 1094: 13–27.

Olson, D.H., C.S. Russel, and D.H. Sprenkle. 1989. *Circumplex model: systematic assessment and treatment of families.* New York: Haworth Press.

Reiss, D. 1980. *Family systems in America.* New York: Holt, Reinhart & Winston.

Rutter, M. 2006. Implications of resilience concepts for scientific understanding. *Annals of the New York Academy of Sciences* 1094: 1–12.

Sampson R., S.W. Raudenbush, and F. Earls. 1997. Neighborhoods and violent crime: a multilevel study of collective efficacy. *Science* 277: 918–24.

Schuster, M.A., B.D. Stein, L.H. Jaycox, R.L. Collins, G.N. Marshall, and M.N. Elliot. 2001. A national survey of stress reactions after September 11 2001 terrorist attacks. *New England Journal of Medicine* 345: 1507–12.

Walsh, F. 2007. Traumatic Loss and major disasters: strengthening family and community resilience. *Family Process* 46, no. 2: 207–27.

An afflicted waiting

Denise A. Peltomaki

Introduction

All of us have experienced suffering in one form or another. We may have suffered through the death of a loved one or the unjust wrath of an employer or teacher; we may have been struck with an illness that demanded more than we felt we could endure. Suffering confronts its victim face to face in the dark alley of despair. We have all suffered, but not all of us have suffered affliction. Indeed, suffering and affliction are not interchangeable terms. They are in the same conceptual family but are not equivalent. Suffering can be understood as a simpler form of affliction, something perhaps that leaves bruises rather than scars. Suffering can be forgotten over time; affliction permeates the soul and affects one's future direction, one's destiny and one's hope. In this essay I portray affliction theoretically and personally to demonstrate that it is an extreme condition; experiencing its wounds without hope of personal transformation is more excruciating than the brokenness of affliction itself. I will examine affliction in order to uncover, tentatively, one way toward spiritual transformation in the midst of its abuse.

In first section of this article, the nature of affliction is elucidated, with special emphasis on its devastating effects, the agony of waiting for the sufferer and the need for words to protest affliction. In the second section, I look at affliction from a Christian perspective, particularly noting the affliction of Jesus of Nazareth and what his sufferings mean for Christ's followers. These connections keep hope alive and make spiritual transformation possible. The third section of this article is a response to the growing awareness – in educational circles – that adults must become comfortable in sharing their own anguish with others. Only when this happens can adults be equipped to hear, understand and respond to the affliction that children communicate in various ways. Succinctly, adults have to tell their own difficult stories before they have ears to hear the pain of children. This is especially important to me; I am an experienced children's pastor. My own affliction, resulting from a motor vehicle accident in 2003, is therefore described.

The nature of affliction

Affliction is the ultimate form of suffering

It is important to distinguish between suffering and affliction. New Testament scholar Ann Jervis presents the following definition of suffering: 'that which is endured in either body, mind or spirit as a result of that which is distressing, injurious, or painful. Such suffering includes pain, death, punishment, hardship, disaster, grief, sorrow, loneliness, injury' (Jervis 2007, 4). Note that Jervis portrays suffering as impacting the mind, body *or* spirit. However, when suffering is experienced in all areas simultaneously, the result is affliction. Simone Weil – a French philosopher – clearly made this distinction. She argued that true affliction harms the body, the mind and the relationships in one's life. Interestingly, Weil did not overtly mention the spiritual in her definition, unlike Jervis above. Dorothee Soelle, a theologian who used Weil's work as the foundation for her own suffering paradigm, states,

> The suffering [one may go] through approaches that which Simone Weil calls affliction, distinguishing it from mere pain and suffering. She analyzes suffering in terms of its three essential dimensions: physical, psychological, and social. 'Affliction' involves all three. Pain that strikes us in only one of these dimensions is not only easier to overcome but, above all, easier to forget. (Soelle 1975, 13)

Most often, when we think of affliction, we are drawn to crises that involve physical torment or anguish: someone receiving a terminal diagnosis, a child born with a physical disability, someone crushed in a car accident. Weil and Soelle argue that affliction does not aim its arrows at only one aspect of our humanity. For affliction to be named the villain that it is, it attacks the entire human condition.

Practical theologian Phil Zylla (2008) agrees with Weil's diagnosis, and Soelle's affirmation of it, yet he noticed the absence of the spiritual in both of their definitions. Zylla suggests a fourth dimension of affliction: spiritual desolation (a dark night of the soul). He argues that in severe affliction, one may feel abandoned by God and believe that his/her connection to a divine Other has been severed. Overall, although Weil, Soelle and Zylla have been thoughtful in articulating these dimensions, we must push further to understand the depths of pain the afflicted experience. This is best done through hearing their stories.

One such story is Simone Weil's; she knew affliction firsthand. Her intellectual appraisal of suffering was predicated on personal experience. In a sense, then, she earned the right to speak about affliction. At the age of 12, Weil began to suffer from migraine headaches that eventually required her to take sick leave from her teaching profession. She was also hospitalised as a young adult for a burn accident, in which she knocked a pot of boiling oil over her left leg. Weil's journey into affliction led her to places most would not set foot. Although she was born into a wealthy family, she felt called to identify with the poor. Weil took a factory job and lived amongst those who survived from paycheck to paycheck. She became an advocate for them. During the last season of her life, she entered into solidarity with their suffering and put herself on the same level, restricting herself to their food rations. Her suffering became so intense she was admitted to hospital and died on 24 August 1943 at the age of 34 (Panichas 1977, 440–1). She understood that affliction had the power to crush the human spirit. Its intensity makes one gasp for breath. Weil stated,

> Affliction is not a psychological state; it is a pulverization of the soul by the mechanical brutality of circumstances. The transformation of a man, in his own eyes, from the human condition into that of a half-crushed worm writhing on the ground is a process, which not even a pervert would find attractive. Neither does it attract a sage, a hero, or a saint. Affliction is something which imposes itself upon a man quite against his will. (Panichas 1977, 462)

Although Weil made choices that she knew would lead her down the path of affliction, the above excerpt demonstrates her awareness that – for most – the choice to suffer is not an option. Affliction comes suddenly and with overwhelming power. It devastates all dimensions of life and leaves its victims feeling powerless. Victims come to believe affliction's lies: that there is no recourse, no escape and no one who will stand with them.

Affliction: from muteness, to lament, to solidarity

If the afflicted try to explain their situation, words fail them. Often there are no words to accompany the depth of their despair. With the onslaught of affliction, one immediately enters a stage of muteness. Weil describes this experience:

> As for those who have been struck the kind of blow which leaves the victim writhing on the ground ... they have no words to describe what is happening to them. Among the people they meet, those who have never had contact with affliction in its true sense can have no idea of what it is, even though they may have known much suffering. (Panichas 1977, 441–2)

Indeed, affliction touches every part of the self, including the voice. As Soelle notes, 'There are forms of suffering that reduce one to silence in which no discourse is possible any longer, in which a person ceases reacting as a human agent' (1975, 68).

In the stage of muteness, groans, cries, screams, and whispers of words strung together (often nonsensical) are interspersed with the silence. These screams and cries mirror the internal struggle and demonstrate that no words exist to express the felt anguish. This is the beginning of lament: cries that protest suffering and demand its end. Ideally – in time – the sufferer finds his/her voice to speak of the horrors experienced. This is an important step, as speaking betrays the longing to connect with people, to join in solidarity with other sufferers. The path from muteness to lament lies before the afflicted, and they discover that this is a slow part of the journey. Finding sounds, groans and words is crucial in order to move through the tunnels and bridges on the road ahead. Extreme suffering brings stagnation; it turns people in on themselves and destroys their ability to communicate (Soelle 1975, 69). Therefore, finding words again is a movement forward. The goal is to tell one's story, to try and speak the unspeakable and so deny affliction victory.

Throughout the struggle, some words and thoughts emerge as questions. Zylla believes that there are three primary questions that the afflicted ask as they travel from muteness to lament, loneliness to community, indifference to compassion. These questions are 'Can you hear me?', 'Can you see me?', and 'Will you come to me?' These highlight the isolating nature of affliction, for at the heart of each question is a longing for social and divine connection. Sufferers need to know that others will hear, see, stand with them in their afflictions. Most might assume the significant questions for the afflicted are 'Why?', 'Why me?', and 'Why now?' In my experience, however, the ultimate question the afflicted ask is, 'How much longer?' The waiting is simply unbearable. All of these questions force us to hear the desperation of the afflicted and their longing for hope, connection and meaning. The questions – once voiced – challenge us to stand in solidarity with them and not turn away.

Waiting is a component of affliction

The agony of waiting. Another aspect of affliction – one that is often forgotten or erroneously viewed as inconsequential – is the waiting in suffering. This waiting is one of the 'sufferings in suffering', partly because there are so many uncertainties about what lies ahead: 'How long will this go on?', 'Can I endure it?', 'What if I can't?', 'Who will come to stay with me?', and 'It's been so long – does God not hear me?' For the afflicted, the period of waiting is often perceived as the most difficult part of the journey. Waiting is not desirable or easy to accept. It offers its own unique agonies that cannot be dismissed or downplayed (e.g. as the calm before the storm). With affliction, one is very much in the storm. Acclaimed Italian author and poet, Cesare Pavese, wrote on the difficulties of the 'suffering in waiting', shortly before committing suicide:

> during the moments that follow [acute suffering], those long moments when one relives the last bout of torture and waits for the next ... The sufferer is always in a state of waiting for the next attack, and the next. The moment comes when the screaming crisis seems preferable to that waiting. The moment comes when he screams needlessly, just to break the flow of time, to feel that *something* is happening. (Pavese 1961, 146)

Waiting is an active and hope-tinged process. After reading the above excerpt, we may ask, 'What good could possibly come from waiting?' It is clearly a devastating process for many sufferers, particularly when they feel powerless to effect change. For most, waiting is seen as a passive and inert process, one that engenders helplessness. In studying affliction, however, I began to see another side of waiting, and became aware of my own misconceptions about it. Catholic author Henri Nouwen painted a picture of waiting, in order to demonstrate that it can be both active and moving. He left an academic career to live and work with those who have intellectual special needs. Some of these individuals – the ones with the most profound special needs – are accustomed to waiting, as they are dependent on caregivers for most of their needs. Nouwen learned to see that

> Those who are waiting are waiting very actively. They know that what they are waiting for is growing from the ground on which they are standing. That's the secret. The secret of waiting is the faith that the seed has been planted, that something has begun. Active waiting means to be present fully to the moment, in the conviction that something is happening where you are and that you want to be present to it. A waiting person is someone who is present to the moment, who believes that this moment is the moment. (Nouwen 1995, 15)

And further, waiting involves motion. Nouwen noticed that

> People who wait have received a promise that allows them to wait. They have received something that is at work in them, like a seed that has started to grow. This is very important. We can really wait only if what we are waiting for has already begun for us. So waiting is never a movement from nothing to something. It is always a movement from something to something more. (Nouwen 1995, 13)

In addition to being an active process, the waiting in suffering is also hope-tinged. Because the future is uncertain, there is a desperate, clinging hope that someone will see and understand the pain, someone will come and 'at least say what the situation is'

(Soelle 1975, 70); and someone will work to bring an end to the suffering. Therefore, 'hopeful despair' is at the heart of the waiting in suffering.

Waiting invites us to experience the other. I believe that waiting invites the afflicted into relationship with the Creator. At first, angry questions may be directed at God; this is healthy. After a while, a sense of promise flickers, a small thought that God is not only in the dark with them, but is leading them through the marshes, around tree stumps and down into valleys, each with its own shadow of death. As one wanders through the waiting season(s) of affliction, a voice emerges within; words emerge to communicate the inner turmoil so that the afflicted move from being mute to crying out a lament.

The brokenness of affliction

When I think of brokenness, I immediately picture an individual who is laying in a foetal position, curled up in a dark corner. Affliction requires much of its victim; its sharp pain cuts deep to the core and causes tears to stream down the face as one lays prostrate. Tears communicate what words cannot say. Tears call out for comfort, solidarity and relief. Weeping is born in the depths of the soul, a most private place. As brokenness is felt, release is found; eyes are fountains of the soul. Tears symbolise each moment of brokenness; scars convey the many moments of affliction that link together, leaving the marks of its brutality. If one falls and breaks a bone, an initial response might produce tears of pain. Later, after the bone heals, a visible fracture will always be seen on the *X*-ray film (a subtle reminder of weakness that remains). A scar signifies a price that was paid, flesh that was torn, a soul that was crushed, life that bled. In terms of our exposure to affliction, every aspect of our human being is stripped bare to reveal that

> Our flesh is fragile; it can be pierced or torn or crushed, or one of its internal mechanisms can be permanently deranged, by any piece of matter in motion. Our soul is vulnerable, being subject to fits of depression without cause and pitifully dependent upon all sorts of objects, inanimate or animate, which are themselves fragile and capricious. Our social personality, upon which our sense of existence almost depends, is always and entirely exposed to every hazard. These ... parts of us are linked with the very centre of our being in such a way that it bleeds for any wound of the slightest consequence which they suffer. (Panichas 1977, 454)

As we think of the injuries of affliction and see scars as permanent reminders of the path we still walk, we found ourselves lying at the foot of the Cross, where a new perspective could be born.

A Christian perspective on affliction

Will I find you in the dark?

'Will I find you in the dark?' This is a question that Billman and Migliore suggest most sufferers ask (1999, 104). It is a powerful question. Afflicted ones need assurance that God will be there in their pain, as they journey through a dark night of the soul. The question reflects a spirit of hopefulness. To ask the question implies there is a hope that, yes, we will find God in the darkness, in the affliction. Earlier I said that an experience is affliction if sufferers experience physical, social, psychological, as well as spiritual pain.

From the Christian perspective, Jesus of Nazareth experienced affliction: he suffered the ultimate bodily harm in his crucifixion (physical), was abandoned by his friends (social), and was disturbed over being forsaken by the Father (psychological). As we concentrate our attention on his brutal death, we see that Jesus asked his own questions: 'At noon, darkness fell across the whole land until three o'clock. At three o'clock Jesus called out with a loud voice, *Eloi, Eloi, lema sabachthan?* which means *My God, my God, why have you abandoned me?*' (Mark 15:33–34) and is spiritual abandonment. During his crucifixion, Jesus did not find the Father in the darkness; he felt completely cut off from his life source. Indeed, many sufferers today also search for God in the darkness and do not find him. This must be acknowledged and taken seriously. To say everyone will find God if they search long enough and have faith ignores the reality that many are exhausted from their search, from crying out to God and receiving no perceivable response. We add to their sufferings by implying that their efforts are insufficient; their faith, inadequate.

Weil sheds light on affliction by taking a spotlight and shining it on the hill of Golgotha, the place where Jesus Christ died. She dispels a romantic notion of suffering and declares that we are at the furthest distance from God in our affliction. As Weil states, 'Men struck down by affliction are at the foot of the Cross, almost at the greatest possible distance from God' (Panichas 1977, 444). This is because, for her, 'Affliction causes God to be absent for a time, more absent than a dead man, more absent than light in the utter darkness of a cell. [It is] a kind of horror that submerges the whole soul' (Panichas 1977, 442). For those looking for hope in the midst of affliction, Golgotha scares us. As noted earlier, Christ felt abandoned by God on that hill and on the cross.

The moment that we choose to stand at the foot of the Cross, the nail pierces our afflictions to the Cross of Christ, and we transcend space and time; we experience the supernatural presence of God. This presence sustains and remains with us. To Weil,

> [t]he man whose soul remains oriented towards God while a nail is driven through it finds himself nailed to the very centre of the universe; the true centre which is not in the middle, which is not in space and time, which is God … In this marvelous dimension, without leaving the time and place to which the body is bound, the soul can traverse the whole space and time and come into the actual presence of God. (Panichas 1977, 452)

Again, for Weil, '[t]here is only one thing that enables us to accept real affliction, and that is the contemplation of Christ's Cross. There is nothing else. That one thing suffices' (Panichas 1977, 464).

The persistence of hope

Only as we lay at the foot of Christ's Cross, surrendering tears and uncovering scars, does the realization dawn that the presence of the Holy Spirit permeates every darkness and affliction. Only then can we fully experience the hope that comes from God. Indeed,

> the biblical vision of hope is the longing for that benign and just sovereignty of God which will right all wrongs and which will finally make our tears cease and give our restless heart its final rest in the merciful arms of God, as when a frightened child sobs for joy in the safe arms of a loving parent. (Beker 1987, 11)

This hope, although fragile, is persistent. It is a genuine hope and the bedrock of assurance. As Moltmann notes, '[g]enuine hope is not blind optimism. It is hope with open eyes, which sees the suffering and yet believes in the future. It is only out of disappointment that hope can become wise' (1980, 14). Hope experienced through affliction becomes wise and leads us to desire healing and restoration but also demands a new life, one transformed by the renewing of hope, 'hope which wants something new, instead of seeking a return to the old' (Moltmann 1980, 6). As Billman and Migliore state,

Those who lament dare to name the brokenness of reality rather than denying it; they refuse to pretend that it is other than it is; they want nothing to do with empty consolations. At the same time, they refuse to resign themselves to the given. Like Rachel mourning for her children who are no more, they refuse to be consoled apart from the transformation not only of their own lives but of a world in pain. (1999, 126)

Indeed, the hope for spiritual transformation through affliction – both for oneself and others – is critical.

The hope for spiritual transformation

What does it mean to be spiritually transformed while experiencing affliction, or as a result of it? What does spiritual transformation look like? Is it an event or a series of events? The expression 'spiritual transformation' is one that can be very intimidating. Some see it as a consequence of discipleship, Bible study and/or a close encounter with the divine. Many regard it as a stepping stone – and predecessor – to spiritual maturity. As we grow in our understanding of what spiritual transformation entails, we will begin to recognise its influence at critical junctures in our own lives.

The first connecting point for spiritual transformation is with the self. As human beings we are each created with a mind, body and soul. We all have personal experiences and unique personalities. The heart of an individual is greatly affected and infected by the dynamics of spiritual transformation. Life change cannot happen unless it touches the innermost part of an individual, since 'spiritual neediness and change is on the inside, in the hidden area of the life that God sees and that we cannot see in ourselves without his help' (Willard 2002, 79).

Spiritual transformation can be grounded on the belief that God connects with humanity in a personal way. I believe that we are all created in the image of God. As we encounter humanity and experience pain, disappointment and emptiness, each soul seeks a saviour and transformation, even in affliction. If we picture a highway, we see an open road, other drivers, speed limits, directional signs and turns. Most of our experiences on the road are predictable; others are surprises. Our vantage point allows us to see what is directly in front of us, giving us advanced warning of traffic flow and overall conditions. We may not see the final destination point – or know exactly where it is – but feeling closer to it, we keep our eyes focused and our hands on the wheel. With this mental picture of life as a journey, we realize that spiritual transformation is not a single event or moment in one's life; it occurs across the lifespan. It happens while encountering surprises, tragedies and pit stops along life's road. Although God oversees each of our personal journeys and enables spiritual transformation, much about God's involvement in affliction is mysterious. What is known is that affliction – more than comfort – is a strong impetus for spiritual transformation.

Although we long to grow, we recognize that spiritual transformation is often painful. As a child grows, his/her bones, muscles and organs require more space to allow for the stretching that gives them strength. Sometimes growth requires patience and flexibility; sometimes it brings loss. For spiritual transformation to occur, we must be open to divine probing and pruning. As Mulholland states, 'we suffer under the illusion that our incompleteness, our brokenness, our deadness is something like a sweater that we can easily unbutton and slip off. It is not that easy. Our brokenness is us' (1993, 2). Often brokenness cripples us and encourages us to hide from the Creator. From a Christian point of view, the

process of being conformed to the image of Christ takes place primarily at the points of our unlikeness to Christ's image ... this can be uncomfortable. We would much rather have ...

spiritual transformation focus on those places where we are pretty well along the way. (Mulholland 1993, 37)

But transformation does not forget the past or skip town. It calls individuals to stand in their pain, loss, frustration, and weakness. For me, this cannot be done without the strength and courage found in Christ. Transformation requires me to stand in him.

Growing up in the church, I am reminded of a song we sang in Sunday school, 'Deep and Wide'. I believe its words describe spiritual transformation. It is a deep process and occurs over the lifetime. It molds the human soul. It reaches to the innermost parts of an individual's joy and pain. It challenges us. It discourages us. It faces pain and refuses to give up. It requires us to stand in Christ, even when we can no longer stand. It is wide. It reaches beyond today. It shows us cliffs that we must jump off in order to continue the journey, waters to wade through, difficult roads to walk along. It reaches beyond us to include others. We find ourselves carpooling and intersecting at different points along the way. We learn from experiencing each other. Spiritual transformation is demanding. Some say it asks too much. It asks for our soul. It requires trust in advance. It commands us to hope, in the midst of affliction. It asks us not to travel alone.

I was a children's pastor for many years. When I look back, I wonder if I was able to hear the children as they tried to tell me about their losses. It is now my firm belief that adults have to tell their own stories of affliction, and listen carefully to the story of affliction itself, to hear the grief that children experience and would like to share with someone.

My story

Sunday, 7 December 2003, was a day that began like all others. With my mind focused on the day ahead, I got in my car and began a seven-minute drive to work. It was a bright day, and the air was cool for a December morning. I turned left, then right, and right again. I continued down the windy residential street that led to the main intersection. The light was green. I continued on my journey, the only thing is, I did not keep going!

Within seconds, I was crushed by a collision. A flash of light, the sound of tires shrieking and metal crushing, the smell of powdered airbags – all of this overwhelmed my senses. It happened so fast, yet it played in my head millisecond by millisecond. My car was struck at the front, and as it spun was hit again at the back end. A driver heading in the opposite direction had gone through a red light. My adrenaline surged; my body began to focus its attention on pain. My left leg was injured. My head was burning. I focused my eyes, and slowed the tape playing over and over in my head, and realised that I was now facing the opposite direction to the path I had been taking. I could not see the other vehicle or driver. After a quick call to 911 and a friend, I turned to my injured knee. I cried. I could not hold back tears. A man in his thirties, who witnessed the accident, came to offer me support. Soon the fire truck came, and emergency workers. Thereafter, I was taken away to Credit Valley Hospital.

As the hospital staff began to focus on my injuries, questions flew in every direction. An exam was given, X-rays taken, tests performed and medication prescribed. As I lay in a quiet, dark cubicle waiting for my X-ray results, listening to monitors and medical staff caring for other patients, tears streamed down my face, and onto my neck. I had been hurt.

Five years later, my life has been a journey of pain and suffering as a result of that car accident. I have endured loss. I have had four surgeries, three on my back (which now has a metal rod and four screws in it). I continue to have severe physical limitations. I wore a back brace for six months, donated my own blood for one of my surgeries, ambulated with the use of a walker, slept in a hospital bed for a year and a half, require the use of medication since the accident, needed over a dozen epidural spinal injections, wear knee and ankle braces, deal with continuing sciatic pain in my left hip and leg, and have partial paralysis in my left foot as a result of nerve damage and scar tissue.

My life is altered. I am not able to work, will not be able to be a children's pastor again, and am not confident that I will be able to return to full-time ministry. I am currently without a salary and have lost my home and my job. I attend physiotherapy at the hospital three days a week and often have several medical appointments per week. I cannot drive more than 10 minutes at a time and cannot drive during rush hour or at night. I am dependent on the services of Transhelp, which provides transportation to and from my appointments. I can hardly begin to comprehend the dynamics of loss, trauma, disappointment, frustration and pain that I have felt and still experience. My afflictions are not merely physical. I face emotional, psychological, social, financial and spiritual challenges from the accident. When I look in the mirror, I see not only physical scars; I see marks that permeate my whole being.

Questions plague me. What is God teaching me? Am I learning? What about my future? Will I be in ministry again? If so, what will it look like? How will my financial and practical needs be met? How do I feel about the affliction I experience? Do I trust God enough for present and future concerns? How can I deal with the effects of the past on my daily life? When will God redeem the pain? I do not have answers or confidence in my understanding of what God is doing. These questions cut me deeply; they challenge my trust in God, others and myself. But I am drawn to two other questions that terrify me: 'Will I find you in the dark?' and 'How much longer?' I still travel along that same rough road.

My hope

I will not candy-coat my experience. Nor will I gloss over my losses. Affliction is a difficult road to travel; I did not volunteer for this. Yet in my affliction, I feel hope rising. I have seen the hand of God. Solidarity with others matters. I am often left speechless as I contemplate gracious mercies extended to me by others. I cannot begin to offer adequate thanks for those who visited me in the hospital, sent cards and gifts, cooked meals and chauffeured me to appointments. Likewise, I will never forget those who offered words of encouragement, packed up my house, moved my belongings, accommodated my educational needs, provided excellent medical care, gave me a roof over my head, and took my name and needs before the Creator of the universe. I never fully appreciated – until my accident – the healing potential of others standing in solidarity with those who suffer, lavishing everyday graces on them.

I am often brought back to the afflictions of Job and drawn to his steadfastness. Although he struggled to perceive God's purposes, he never rejected or cursed his Maker. His bedrock held in the storms of life and offered hope during wretched moments. But hope is difficult to articulate. It is not dependant on feelings, perceptions or strategies. It is not based on security in possessions or status. With Moltmann, I now see hope as more than feeling, more than experience, more than foresight. Hope is a command. Obeying hope enables me to live, survive, endure, and stand up to life until death is swallowed up in victory. Obeying hope means never giving way to forces of annihilation that inhere in affliction or giving in to resignation and rage (Moltmann 1980, 20). Moltmann went further in describing hope. As he witnessed, first-hand, the horrors of the Second World War, he expanded his view of hope by saying,

> Men and women are called to enduring hope. True hope is not based on the ebb and flow of our feelings. Nor does it come from success in life. True hope – which means the hope that

endures and sustains us – is based on God's call and command. We are called to hope. It is a command: a command to resist death. It is a call: the call to divine life ... Enduring hope is not something innate, something we possess from birth. Nor do we acquire it from experience. We have to learn it. We learn to hope if we obey the call. We learn to hope in the experiences life brings us. We come to know its truth if we are forced to stand our ground against despair. We come to know its power when we realize that it keeps us alive in the midst of death. (Moltmann 1980, 19)

Affliction strikes hard. It crushes bones, draws blood, cuts deep, pulverises the soul, beats down, whips, trips, kicks, pierces and neglects. It buries an individual alive; beats us until we cannot be recognised. As I contemplate hope and the Cross, I am welcomed into Christ's presence. I am invited to stay, to touch the holes in his hands, to feel the torn flesh on his side, and to see the love in His eyes. As I look, I am struck by Christ's affliction. I weep. I cannot speak. I cannot move. His voice calls me to stand, yet I cannot. He calls me again to stand, but not to stand in myself – to stand in him. He bends to my level. In my weakness, he gently helps me to rise. As muscles, ligaments and bones straighten, I find myself face to face with the lover of my soul. He touches my scars one at a time and says he is sorry I have to endure such pain. In this moment, I have hope that transcends the brokenness of affliction.

I hope that, because of my experience of tragedy and my telling of it, I will be able to help others in their grief. Perhaps I will play a role in helping others to stand again after suffering great loss, including children.

Conclusion

The purpose of this article was to say that ultimate suffering – affliction – has physical, social, psychological and spiritual dimensions. Sufferers move from muteness to lament, ideally at least, until they regain solidarity with others. It is my belief that a process of waiting, for those that suffer, and the persistence of hope, can have a spiritually transforming effect on the afflicted. In the end, because affliction is pervasive, sufferers have to learn to tell their stories as part of the healing process. Only then can they truly hear – and respond to – the stories of loss that others try to convey. This is as true for children as it is for adults. And it is why, as a former children's pastor who has experienced great loss, I told my own story of affliction.

References

Beker, C.J. 1987. *Suffering and hope: The biblical vision and the human predicament.* Philadelphia: Fortress.

Billman, K.D., and D.L. Migliore. 1999. *Rachel's cry: Prayer of lament and rebirth of hope.* Cleveland, OH: United Church Press.

Jervis, A. 2007. *At the heart of the gospel: Suffering in the earliest Christian message.* Grand Rapids, MI: Eerdmans.

Kubler-Ross, E. 1983. *On children and death.* New York: Simon and Schuster.

Moltmann, J. 1980. *Experiences of God.* London: SCM.

Mulholland, Jr, M.R. 1993. *Invitation to a journey*. Downers Grove, IL: InterVarsity.
Nouwen, H.J.M. 1995. *The path of waiting*. New York: Crossroad.
Panichas, G.A., ed. 1977. *The Simone Weil reader*. New York: David McKay Company, Inc.
Pavese, C. 1961. *This business of living: Diaries, 1935–1950*. London: Peter Owen Ltd.
Soelle, D. 1975. *Suffering*. Philadelphia: Fortress.
Willard, D. 2002. *Renovation of the heart*. Colorado Springs, CO: NavPress.
Zylla, P. 2008. Theology of suffering class. January-April, Ontario, Canada.

Pastor Emile's children

Emile Desmond Ebun Sam-Peal

Introduction

People who see the movie *Blood diamond* get a glimpse of Liberia. The country is in a state of extreme poverty, following almost 20 years of civil warfare. As a result, its infrastructure is crushed. Monrovia is scraped to its concrete bones. Five-star hotels are indistinguishable in the city's ruins. Many streets are rendered nearly impassable. The holes in these roads were left by artillery fire; they were blown up by rebels to prevent Liberians from escaping the city. Rebels were able to create conditions in which the freedom of movement was almost eliminated. At this point, personnel from the United Nations Mission in Liberia are policing checkpoints and rebuilding roads as they hold together an uneasy peace by the sheer force of numbers.

There are few places for Liberians to live. Many families share protection under thin, loosely woven mats that cover the family at night, mats that fail to keep out mosquitoes that plague the whole of Africa (Sachs 2006, 198–9) so that malaria is a constant threat. People lack rudimentary shelter to keep the rain out of the hut, a chimney to remove smoke from a cook stove, and essential clothing, such as shoes (Sachs 2006, 19–20). Some people live in the remnants of government or business buildings gutted by fire or destroyed by shelling. Schools and other public facilities were destroyed or so seriously damaged they are unusable. Utilities such as electricity and water services are limited. Commerce was undermined, as was farming. It may seem odd to those that have never experienced extreme disruption, but people forget how to carry out ordinary tasks of living when civility collapses, as it did in Liberia: people forget how to farm and tend the soil (Jacobs 1984, 124; Diamond 2006). In Liberia's case, rubber trees were destroyed; other industries floundered, though the country is rich with natural resources.

Extreme poverty is a trap characterised by disease, physical isolation, climate stress and environmental degradation, so that households cannot meet basic needs for survival. Families are chronically hungry, unable to secure health care, have no access to safe drinking water and sanitation, and cannot afford education for all their children.

The eruption of extreme poverty is an outcome of rebel fighting. Since 1980 there has been a series of events that left Liberia politically, socially and economically unstable. Before his assassination in 1980, President Tolbert had a high profile as a Baptist leader as well as a political leader. He also served as president of the Baptist Convention and participated actively in Baptist World Alliance leadership. Hence, in the early days of political change after Tolbert's assassination, there were new leaders that linked the Baptist community with former political alliances, a connection that resulted in suspicion towards all Baptists. The alienation of Baptists has dissipated over time, with the realisation that events were precipitated by political rather than religious motives. Over the decades since 1980, the country endured military dictatorships as well as elections that put in place former military dictator Samuel Doe, and later, rebel leader Charles Taylor. Currently Charles Taylor is being tried at the Hague for crimes against humanity. Estimates point to over 300,000 people killed during his regime. The current government is headed by President Ellen Johnson Sirleaf, the first female head of state to be elected in an African country.

Throughout the rebel wars, children suffered enormous losses in terms of family members massacred before their eyes; they lost any sense of personal security, and many were forced to become child soldiers, kept at war by being starved, on the one hand, and fed drugs, on the other. The sense of unreality that children experience is conveyed by stories that circulate throughout the country. As one example, when UN troops entered Liberia to end the rebel domination, one armoured tank crew became aware of two young boys shooting at their vehicle, using small guns. Unfortunately, the boys were killed when army personnel fired back because the boys would not stop shooting. As UN soldiers went over to them, they were shocked to see how young these boys were and also discovered that the boys' pockets were stuffed with drugs.

For child soldiers, as well as for the children who were their victims, education is a significant need. At present, most children get to schools *via* taxis. The current minister of transportation, Honourable Jeremiah Sulunteh has an overwhelming portfolio: in order for children to go to school they need roads and transportation. Even when some Liberians begin to farm again, in order for them to transport their products, roads need to be redeveloped and communication facilities must be restored or rebuilt. As is evident, extreme poverty creates a web of problems; the instability of each aspect of social, political and cultural life threatens the attempt to address any of the others.

While Liberia is seriously damaged by the civil crisis, the current moment is one of hope based on the people's capacity for resilience. There is a new government that seems to have people's confidence. Driving through the countryside, one notices renewal and rebuilding since the time Ellen Johnson Sirleaf became president. African countries have risen again, despite poverty and warfare. As an example of that hope, the nearby country of Ghana was unstable and subject to significant poverty 20 years ago and is now economically buoyant and enjoys a viable political and economic infrastructure. However, Ghana has a history of 50 years of relative stability and was not decimated by rebel warfare as Liberia has been.

One of the pressing educational and spiritual problems Liberia faces is the troubled relationships among people who were on both sides of the rebel warfare and who now must find a way to live together in that small country. In particular, the sheer number of orphans and street children is staggering, as is the number of child soldiers who are now ex-combatants and have unique problems of adjustment. In response to the whole complex of problems that Liberia faces, the author has chosen to work with children. He was the leader of a large Christian denomination (Baptist) throughout most of the rebel warfare and took up the plight of all these children.

Human responses

The author worked with groups of children during the war and in its aftermath. It was a time when social services to communities in Liberia were almost nonexistent. Stories are still told by adults who come upon a small cluster of coconut fruit (nuts) on the ground and they recall how several years ago, during the fighting, they would have taken such a treasure and buried it to provide them with a few days of food. Several pine nuts might be all they had for a whole day, if they were fortunate to find them. If adults were forced to hunt and gather in this way, many children and youth also had to fend for themselves, making them vulnerable to crime and violence.

The author's program was geared to children and youth between the ages of 6 to 25 years. He tried to develop the Children's Resource Network (CRN) as an organisation to provide care, guidance and resources to meet the needs of children and youth, one of the most vulnerable groups during times of cultural chaos. He saw they were abused, drugged, and turned into killing machines, then used to kill, maim, and rape civilians. Since they were perceived as mere instruments in rebel hands, many were killed. Survivors have life but were denied a normal childhood. Many were orphaned or abandoned, and they continue to search for a community and connection to something to provide emotional and physical sustenance. While the CRN is not fully functioning, in his effort to initiate the program the author worked with many children and youth. The stories that follow give evidence of the hope that they will one day enjoy the ordinary pleasures of life.

Using Dr Martin Luther King Jr's famous phrase, *I have a dream*, he asked the children to write down their dreams. He kept many of them; some of their responses are found in what follows:

I have a dream that one day I will be a doctor
I have a dream that I will treat the whole world in times of illness
I have a dream that the Liberian government will fix the roads
I have a dream that buses will be provided for schools
I have a dream that one day we will live in a peaceful land
I have a dream

By Koc W.

I have a dream that one day all children will go to school and they will have good food to eat
I have a dream that money will be given in order to clean our streets and have lights
I have a dream

By Nekula F.

I have a dream that all children will go to school in Liberia
I have a dream that one day there will be more food in Liberia
I have a dream that lights will be everywhere
I have a dream

By Prosper

I have a dream that there will be more, better food and water
I have a dream that one day everybody, the poor and the rich, will have the same clothes to wear

By Dominique

I have a dream that all people will send their children to good schools
I have a dream that all people will give their children good food to eat, so they can grow healthy
I have a dream that all children will have clothes to wear and a better place to sleep

By Matenneh K.

I have a dream that one day Liberians will respect one another
I have a dream that Liberians will one day help build their country
I have a dream that one day there will be good schools in Liberia

By Paul E.

I have a dream that one day children will no longer sell in the streets but go to better schools
I have a dream that one day there will be more food in Liberia and lights all over the city of Monrovia
I have a dream that roads and bridges will be built in Liberia

By Sada K.

The following brief letter to the author, affectionately known as 'Pastor Bobo' by children in his care, is one indication of the needs children have to receive assistance in the context of a caring community:

Dear Pastor Bobo,

Beloved greetings to you and all the wonderful people that came to visit us.

May God bless you for all the help you give me. Now I can play, run, and be like other children. You are a gift sent to help a lonely child. I am now well and back in school. I don't know what to say for what you did for me. Again I want to say may thanks and may God bless you all. I pray that one day we will see you people again. I love you. Smile. I love you. I miss you and pray every day for you people.

My favourite Bible verse is taken from the book of Psalms 107:1 – 'Oh, give thanks unto the Lord for he is good, for his mercy endureth forever'.

Your lonely daughter,

Josephine S.

The hopes reflected in these heart-felt poems, as well as the letter, demonstrate that children everywhere long for stability and opportunity, even in the face of devastating experiences. Paying attention to their needs and doing something to respond and remain connected to them, however small the effort may seem, offers them a chance to begin rebuilding their lives and future. Progress may be slow, but children are resilient, and they are grateful for the care and the effort on their behalf by the adults who surround them.

Acknowledgements

The stories of these children are used by permission. We express our gratitude to them and wish them well.

References

Diamond, J. 2006. *Collapse: How societies choose to fail or succeed.* New York: Penguin.
Jacobs, Jane. 1984. *Cities and the wealth of nations.* New York: Vintage.
Sachs, Jeffrey D. 2006. *The end of poverty.* London: Penguin.

Linking spirituality, school communities, grief and well-being

Louise Rowling

Introduction

The focus for this article is on the school community as the people and place where loss and learning occur. In the last decades, school communities globally face events that present significant spiritual and psychosocial challenges as a result of global terrorism and violence that are part of everyday life. Exposure to events through onsite media coverage and the targeting by terrorists of previously safe environments, such as schools, has changed trauma and grief from a private experience to a shared community phenomenon. Due to the intimacy of media coverage, grief may be the outcome of first-hand experience or a vicarious reaction to others' suffering. In response to the communal aspect, I explore loss and grief in school communities to exemplify the importance of people and place for the well-being of children and youth.

To acknowledge the linkages between people and place in the health of the young, I note a resonance among the primary concepts of spirituality, loss, grief, supportive school communities, mental health and well-being. Theoretical and conceptual linkages among these terms rely on related ideas used in this article, such as assumptive world views (the collection of assumptions that form one's identity and view of the world); connectedness (relationality); meaning making; and a sense of place (the positive value environments have for individuals and groups). The primary concepts are drawn together by illustrating how they frame a health perspective on spirituality, loss, grief and well-being in the context of schools. I rely on the primary concepts as I explore strategies that create healthy whole school communities, i.e. ones that address loss and grief in a way that promotes well-being in the young. I discuss the primary concept of spirituality and outline the strategies I recommend from my own research that help to form a whole school community capable of dealing with loss and grief.

Spirituality

There is a diversity of views about what constitutes spirituality. Its elements that are the focus of this article are meaning-making, purpose in life, and connectedness to people and places. This choice is an outcome of a number of research studies on loss and grief that I conducted in school communities and with university students. Frequently, young people and teachers have reported that a major loss prompts them to think about the meaning of life and their place in it; and one key experience is feeling supported within their community by others.

   The concept of spiritual health is also of increasing interest to health professionals. It has been argued that the spiritual dimension of health provides the meaning and purpose in life and acts as a unifying force within an individual, which integrates other dimensions of health (Rowling and Gehrig 1998). In this view, spiritual health is seen as

> the product of connectedness to self, to others and a greater reality. Balance and harmony of these three areas of connectedness create optimal spiritual health and the conditions to achieve one's full potential in life. (Gehrig 1998, 46)

As well, the World Health Organisation Quality of Life measure (WHOQOL Group 1998), in its assessment of what makes life worth living, measures mental, social and spiritual well-being. By examining the contribution of all three dimensions to an overall ranking of quality of life, linkages are made between a lack of mental distress, relationships with others, various spiritual variables and overall happiness and well-being. Benson and colleagues (2003) emphasise connectedness in their concept of spiritual development. They see spirituality as

> the developmental 'engine' that propels the search for connectedness, meaning, purpose and contribution. It is shaped both within and outside of religious traditions, beliefs and practices. (205)

De Souza and Hyde (2007) argue that the concept of relationality (my term, connectedness), involves good and effective relationships. There is strong support for the importance of connectedness in social-support research literature. Cohen and Syme (1985) emphasise the importance of connectedness with others that gives an increased sense of meaning and social well-being. Likewise Bellingham and colleagues (1989) describe the ability to live in the wholeness of life, identifying connectedness as a key process that can be enhanced by exploring how well one is connected to oneself, to others, and to some large meaning or purpose. Similarly, de Souza and Hyde (2007) in their summarising of the research and thinking about spirituality and young people argue that spirituality

> covers a range of areas that relate to connectedness that a young person may feel to self, community and, perhaps, something beyond; the resilience that becomes apparent in times of

great stress and struggle; the notions of identity and the, sometimes, associated rites of passage; the development of values and meaning-making; and finally, the role of spirituality in mental and social health and well-being. (97)

In this research, relationality among human persons is posited as a key component of spirituality that also contributes to well-being. As a further example, well-being in de Souza and Hyde's definition was elaborated by Richard Eckersley (2004), where he argues that it hinges upon 'being connected and engaged, from being suspended in a web of relationships and interests: personal, social and spiritual. This gives meaning to our lives' (23).

In terms of its connection to schools and schooling, in Australia the concept of spirituality was included in the National Goals of Schooling (MCEETYA 1999, 1), which states that 'Schooling provides a foundation for young Australian's intellectual, physical, social, moral, spiritual and aesthetic development'. Despite its inclusion in the statement, Hodder (2007) argues that little has been done so far in the secular government education system, except to support spirituality in the National Goal 1.3, which states that when students leave school they should

have the capacity to exercise judgement and responsibility in matters of morality, ethics and social justice, and the capacity to make sense of their world, to think about how things got to be the way they are, to make rational and informed decisions about their own lives and to accept responsibility for their own actions. (MCEETYA 1999, 2)

But these goals are not placed within context. As Hodder (2007) explains, they 'are anti-contextual because they are promoted in isolation from a holistic perspective and separated from a person's cognitive, social, emotional and spiritual development' (183).

A whole school community approach insists on an holistic inclusion of spirituality, based on researching common themes of spirituality that imply a relationship between connectedness and well-being. The approach also resonates with the public health approach to loss and grief in schools that is presented in the next section. I introduce and recommend a shift in practice from an individualistic to a community focus as a way to ground strategies for forming whole school communities described in sections that follow this next part.

Loss, grief and schools: its problems and a shift in practice

In many school environments the current individualised approach to intervening with grieving young people focuses on providing counselling services to individual students or groups of students and in some cases outside referral to doctors who may prescribe medication as part of a treatment regime. In this way young people are seen as having a problem (being bereaved), and action focuses on fixing the problem.

A different way of viewing this situation occurs when it is examined through the lens of a public health approach to loss and grief in schools (Rowling 2003). Such an approach focuses on the school community and how conditions can be created and enhanced that assist students as well as school personnel in student support roles. Creating this supportive place can provide a normalising and affirming environment (Johnson 1989). The 'normality' of school routines establishes these conditions. The normality is not just 'business as usual' in time of crisis but uses the structures of schools – of personal interactions, time schedules and pastoral care networks – as a framework for effective support. In this way various types of support are offered.

When support operates in a whole school community, emotional support arises from actions focused on individuals such as the acknowledgement of feelings of sadness so that children are allowed time out from lessons and/or providing opportunities to express those feelings in art, writing or through vigorous physical activity. Social support comes from the sense of communal caring and connectedness in shared rituals, or from school structures such as special grief support groups conducted in the school. Practical support for a bereaved teacher could come from colleagues who take his or her classes and extra duties, or from school practices that allow staff to take an informal leave during periods of grief. It is through organisational practices of the school that people are provided with support as well as from school personnel that are available day-to-day within that community.

Working strategically to achieve a holistic public health approach to bereavement in school communities requires a reorientation of current approaches from outside agencies to service delivery. This reorientation may include asking support providers who work with schools to shift from acting solely as grief experts to become facilitators and supporters of the actions of school personnel (Rowling 2005), so that they create proactive partnerships with school communities. It also requires school community members and parents to recognise a critical role the school, as a social institution, can play in times of crisis. Such an approach is concerned about safety and predictability in the school environment, for learning to be optimised. It is an organisational and structural approach that uses the strengths of the school community to restore safety and security in the learning worlds of the young.

Supportive school communities

A supportive whole school community approach starts with a school perspective rather than an individual or service provider viewpoint. This requires a focus not just on student needs but also on what all school community members need and what the school as an *organisation* needs in order to enhance the environment so that it is supportive of loss and grief. This is required because many young people, because of family or community taboos, grieve silently and alone, while others may look to peers and teachers in their schools for help that

- Assists in defining the reality of their loss
- Allows expression of feelings associated with it to validate their experience
- Provides support and access to information
- Assists integration of the experience into their lives to restore a sense of safety and security.

These needs are met within the school community context with outside support.

A whole school approach is proactive and comprehensive, since it is underpinned by the following principles. Firstly, there needs to be acceptance that the social context impacts on the meaning of loss events in people's lives. A school crisis needs to be managed within the context of the school, ideally by school personnel with outside support. Existing school history and culture helps to provide a framework for making-meaning; as an example, the particular history of a previous crisis event in the school, whether it was handled well or badly, will influence the school community as it addresses subsequent events. School members are the ones that know this history. Secondly, grief should be seen as a normal life event that can be managed by school communities with outside support; it should not be pathologised and seen as only the domain of outside experts. Thirdly, since people react differently to loss experiences, we cannot prescribe steps one to five nor expect particular behaviour, such as anger, will occur. This predictive approach is not helpful. There is a range of behaviours that people exhibit and each person will experience and express them differently. Fourthly, there are different strategies that help students and teachers cope with their own and/or their friends' loss experiences. Fifthly, school policies, practices and partnerships as well as individual actions maximise effective management. We need to adopt an organisational as well as an individual orientation. And finally, all school community members may need support if a death occurs in a school.

To effectively support all school community members, several strategies are needed that are based on the recognition of a wider framework for grief experiences. This wider framing facilitates understanding the impact these events have on school community members when their sense of security in their everyday lives is disrupted and when events disturb their assumptive world of schools being safe places. Using a more comprehensive framework for taking action in response to loss and grief, a whole school community needs an ethos that enfranchises, validates, and restores the quality of life among its membership that includes students, teachers and school leaders (i.e. principals, head teachers).

Enfranchising school communities

A school needs to be an enfranchising community. That is, it needs to be a community that minimises the occurrence of disenfranchised grief. Disenfranchised grief refers to 'the grief that persons experience when they incur a loss that is not or cannot be openly acknowledged, publicly mourned, or socially supported' (Doka 1989, 4; 2002, 10). There are five triggers for disenfranchised grief:

- The relationship that embodies the loss is not recognised
- The loss itself is not recognised
- Society does not give the person the role of one who is grieving
- The specific circumstances of the loss
- The different ways individuals grieve.

As one example, a relationship that embodies loss that is unrecognised is the death of a boy's grandfather, if he provided the companionship that an absent father did not provide and the school did not know about this relationship.

There are a number of sources of disenfranchised grief in a school community – intrapersonal (self), interpersonal (others) and environmental (the social world of the school). Intrapersonal sources include fear generated by perceived social disapproval; fear of loss of losing personal control (linked to the importance of feelings of independence); and the current perceptions and interpretations of their world that it is an environment that does not permit them to express loss openly (Rowling 2002). In particular, boys and young men are subject to disenfranchisement resulting from the varying ways they process their grief, at both intra- and interpersonal levels.

As an example, a 13-year-old boy, in discussing the death of his uncle, reported that he had witnessed another boy being teased; he also reported his reaction to the boy that was teased (Rowling 2002, 283). The grieving boy came back to school after his dad died from cancer. The 13 year old, whose uncle recently died, reported that the boy whose father died

> came back to school and this older kid gave him some crap about it. He went off crying. *You are better leaving them alone when that happens* [my emphasis]. It is not good standing there watching them crying *making them think* 'Oh God I'm a wimp! So I kept quiet.

As the narrative indicates, words and actions of students towards a grieving peer may prompt a form of self censorship due to what students have already witnessed at school.

It is important to recognise that there are gendered behaviour patterns (Martin and Doka 2000) that might also be the source of disenfranchised grief. Young men may not talk about their experiences and feelings, but they are still processing and organising their thoughts; as Ricardo said,

> It is good to hear what others are saying. You can just sit there and listen and *you have a conversation with yourself, in your mind*, you turn it over and that helps. It gives you ideas about how you might explain yourself if you were in that situation. (Rowling 2002, 287; my emphasis)[1]

What is needed in school environments is an acceptance of the varying ways to express grief so that the community sanctions these options for young males that they may process grief by taking action rather than through the verbal expression of their feelings, and by thinking it through rather than talking about it with others.

Validating loss experiences

If sources of disenfranchisement inhibit healthy diverse expressions of grief, it is particularly important that teachers and school leaders are part of a grieving community that, through its structures and processes, minimises disenfranchised grief. Validating school communities are ones that have a proactive comprehensive approach, with policies, structures and action plans in place to be used when needed, which all the school members know about, especially teachers and leaders. For teachers to acknowledge their personal and professional reactions to crises in schools is an essential occupational health and safety issue. That is, they may control their reactions in their professional roles, but be deeply affected personally.

This duality between inward responses and outward expression is a key element in the identification of teachers as disenfranchised grievers (Rowling 1995). Disenfranchised grief in teachers is created by their personal/professional duality, in which they may be pulled between their need to be 'human', their professional beliefs around the duty of care for young people and between being in personal and professional control. A teacher, Guy, recounts that,

> When you confront these big issues, like death, the fact that they are young kids, it really spins you around and next time you want to be prepared for that, it's very painful for yourself, plus you want to, as a teacher, be there for the kids. (Rowling 1995, 323)

Teaching is a profession where emotional connections are made; it is based on human interaction. Teachers care for their pupils. They hold the assumption that they have to hide their emotions in order to manage a class. When death occurs, there is a real fear of 'breaking down' in front of the class. If something traumatic happens, it is likely to involve their intense emotional response. These may be emotions they had not fully recognised in themselves.

Being affected by grief influences teachers' beliefs as competent professionals, due to the need to feel they have control of the situation. When events occur that challenge their professional beliefs, the assumptive world of the teacher is shaken. They may feel they will let down their students and that their emotional response will affect their occupational future, as well as the well-being of young people in their care. The tension between being in control and being human is a key concern in this role conflict (Rowling 1995). Teachers need an environment that recognises and validates their grief and that provides support for it.

So, uniquely for the teaching profession, their grief can be disenfranchised by this personal professional conflict created by their need to maintain their humanity as part of their teaching role: their professional beliefs about what behaviour is appropriate and their duty of care for young people. Grief creates a role conflict, within which 'control' and 'being human' are key concerns, especially if the environment of the school does not recognize this and establish processes that validate their reactions and beliefs.

In the experience of school leaders, there are some similar beliefs about their role but also some assumptions that are distinctively connected to the role as leader. Principals or Head teachers experience a complex interweaving of themselves in their professional role and themselves as human beings, in their own minds as well as in the minds of school community members (Rowling 2003). For one group of leaders, there was a divide between the personal and professional – a dichotomy particularly in relation to whether or when emotions should be expressed. Another group felt that there was not such a clear division: it had more to do with what should be kept private, which personal characteristics were part of a professional tone they felt was important. In both groups, assumptions were made about what is personal, what is professional, and what of the personal self is allowed to impact on the professional. These assumptions moved leaders to declare that a particular response had nothing to do with the professional life, so that it was kept separate and kept private.

A third group saw no distinction between the personal and the professional. For example, Mike a school principal, recounted a critical incident in his school (Rowling 2003, 98). He asked,

> What do you say, when you walk into a distraught, absolutely distraught man in front of you? He has the counsellor on one side and the chaplain the other. The father looks me in the eyes and says, 'Mr. M, my boy was so proud of your school and now you've lost him!' I'll never forget those words. I represent the school. That's when it hits! It hits hard. Yes, you do represent the school. It is your school. They do attach it personally to you. You're the man at the top that makes it all happen. I don't quite know what I did say, something about 'I am very sorry' I guess. That was a very difficult day, a very difficult day.

As part of the third group, Mike acknowledged the impact of a school boy's death on him personally. Yet for other leaders, the emotional impact of grief events is downplayed or ignored. As one example, Phillip said, the feeling

> just never leaves you. It has certainly never left me. And I do think it is of such a significance, well it was to me personally … I felt it so deeply, it could have been the finish of me.

This incident was so stressful that Phillip took sick leave. The above comments were made four years after the event. At that time Phillip did not allude to the need to take sick leave.

Whatever action a leader takes, he or she may encounter disputes with parents about age appropriateness of discussions about death and on the other hand may receive criticism from staff about returning the school to normal instead of having those discussions and giving the students time out to talk about their reactions. Leaders may be harassed by the media, and be so overwhelmed personally they question their competency as a professional.

As one leader reported, there can be great personal challenges when confronted by trauma. Andrew noted that

I suppose the hard thing is not coming to terms with the fact of what Jim had done [committed suicide], but really coming to terms with my inability to comfort the father. You expect that as a human being, if another human being is suffering you might be able to ease the pain. But in this first encounter that was exceedingly difficult.

The lack of support that a principal experiences from the larger school system is a mitigating factor that overarches the management of crisis events.

From an organisational perspective, it is essential to create a workplace that validates and enfranchises the experience and expression of grief for all school personnel, and it is helpful if the system within which the school operates also validates loss and the grieving process. Within the school, teachers and leaders have another way to validate grief through educating their students. In a whole school community, the aim of education is more than exploring the feelings of grief (see Ward and Houghton 1988): it involves developing competencies. These competences combine knowledge and practical skill so that learners gain

- Knowledge about loss and grief reactions
- Skills to use the information to help themselves
- Knowledge and skills to seek help and recognise when support would be beneficial, particularly for 'instrumental grievers' (also known as masculine grievers; Martin and Doka 2000)
- Information about loss experiences to understand and support others
- Knowledge and skills about loss and grief to assist students to be a supportive school community member so that they understand grief, thereby the 'difference' a grieving young person may experience can be minimised (Rowling 2000, 9).

To validate and enfranchise grief in schools there needs to be a critical examination of beliefs and assumptions about, and the rules for, grieving, as well as an understanding of professional roles. For example, if school leaders understand their role comprehensively, they can by their reactions and behaviour provide guidance for the community's response especially if there is confusion, anger and doubt. Their considered action can create a social world that sanctions various forms of grieving behaviour.

Where an event has affected large numbers of school community members, the meaning of a crisis needs to be collectively created. This meaning-making is a deliberate act that helps individuals in a school community to make sense of the event by talking it through and telling their stories. Community sharing creates a sense of predictability in the emotional, physical, social and spiritual world of the school. For older adolescents this may include existential questioning and uncertainty about their religious beliefs.

Restorative communities

There is a different need in schools when the loss is a result of violence invading not only individual lives but the entire geographical area and the social space of the school. In this instance, there is a violation of the sense of safety in the school itself. School members' assumptive worlds of feeling safe disappear and need to be recreated. Actions need to be taken to reclaim the school as a safe environment where order, structure and predictability facilitate the daily routines of teaching and learning. These reclaiming rituals allow for feelings to be collectively constructed and expressed. These community rituals create a space, a structure with boundaries, where school community members can feel it is possible to express their tears or reflect on their inner sadness. It is also a place where a sense of hope and faith in the future can be initiated.

In one example, Matt, a school principal, was interviewed about his management of critical incidents. He described the feeling he had when he walked into his school grounds after a young man, unconnected to the school community, had hanged himself in the playground (Rowling 2005). He said that,

> They [the school community] felt very, very intruded upon. And the gravity of having someone commit suicide where you spend a lot of your time pumping emotional energy into, it is very, very difficult. Adults had to reclaim the place for the kids and that was my role to start the process of reclaiming the place for the school community. (168)

After a crisis, individuals need to re-connect with the geographic space and re-construct its identity as a safe school environment.

In general, as a result of violent intrusive events, existing worldviews are challenged but new learning can occur as a result of these experiences. According to Kolto-Rivera (2004, 3), the term worldview comes from the German *Weltanschauung* and refers to a view or perspective on the world or the universe used to describe one's larger outlook on life, society and its institutions. A worldview is a set of assumptions about physical and social reality (Weber et al. 2007). For many school community members, assumptions about their work or learning worlds are connected with their total outlook on life and their spiritual views. To engage in collective action allows students to express grief, the school community to reclaim violated spaces and therefore to re-position the school in a worldview as a safe environment. Memories of connectedness and safety generated by rituals created by students and other school community members are not only healing at the time, they can provide reassurance long after the ceremonies have occurred so that they support new learning.

Mental health and well-being

Fear and loss of security are two mental health problems that are increasing in prominence. Jean Twenge (Twenge 2000) analysed data on young people in the United States over a 60-year period and noted rising anxiety. She describes its occurrence in terms of free-floating anxiety and argues that anxiety is more commonplace than depression. She also found that young people have a lower sense of control over their lives (Twenge 2000). The school is part of student's identity and their overall view of themselves. Loss experiences at school may result in fear, uncertainty, loss of control, and increased anxiety. Active involvement in school rituals can start the process of regaining a sense of control and thereby contribute to a reduction in feelings of fear and uncertainty. Spiritual health as connectedness to people and places can increase an individual's overall sense of well-being. It may act as a unifying force linking dimensions of physical, social and emotional health (Rowling and Gehrig 1998).

Conclusion

Throughout this article, themes have been explored that resonate with spirituality such as meaning making, connectedness and well-being. I have proposed that a whole school approach to loss, grief and mental health supports well-being in children and adolescents. It empowers their relationships and enhances a sense of personal control over their worlds.

Interconnectedness among these dimensions of human experience, summarised by the term spirituality, needs to be acknowledged in school environments.

While intensive research and theorising on specific aspects of children and adolescents' spirituality, health and well-being is essential, so too are the mechanisms for bringing these bodies of knowledge together. In this article, I argued that this can occur in two ways. Firstly, by focusing on the total school environment, that is, both its people and the physical and social place it occupies. This holistic view of schools and its potential positive impact on the young utilises the processes of identification with physical space and the people in this social world. Another mechanism of bringing bodies of knowledge together is through conceptual linking. This article illustrates the process in identifying associations among spirituality, loss, grief, mental health and well-being within the social context of schools. A whole school approach links a sense of connectedness to the processes of meaning-making that allow children and youth to gain insight into the social, emotional and intellectual aspects of their daily school lives.

Note

1. Pseudonyms are used throughout in reporting the interviews used in this article.

References

Bellingham, R., B. Cohen, T.C. Jones, L. Spaniol. 1989. Connectedness: Some skills for spiritual health. *American Journal of Health Promotion* 4, no. 1: 18–25.
Benson, P.L., E.C. Roehlkepartain, and S.P. Rude. 2003. Spiritual development in childhood and adolescence: Toward a field of inquiry. *Applied Developmental Science* 7: 204–12.
Cohen, S., and L. Syme. 1985. *Social support and health.* Orlando, FL: Academic Press.
de Souza, M., B. Hyde. 2007. Spirituality of children and young people: A consideration of some perspectives and implications from research contextualized by Australia. *International Journal of Children's Spirituality* 12, no. 2: 97–104.
Doka, K. 1989. *Disenfranchised grief. Recognising hidden sorrow.* Lexington, MA: Lexington Books.
———. 2002. *Disenfranchised grief: New directions, challenges and strategies for practice.* Champaign, IL: Research Press.
Eckersley, R. 2004. *Well and good: How we feel and why it matters.* Melbourne: Text Publishing.
Gehrig, S. 1998. A study of the spiritual health of Australian adolescents. Paper presented at Education, Spirituality and the Whole Child Conference, June, Froebel Institute, London.
Hodder, J. 2007. Young people and spirituality: The need for a spiritual foundation for Australian schooling. *International Journal of Children's Spirituality,* 12, no. 2: 179–90.
Johnson, K. 1989. *Trauma in the lives of children.* Claremont, CA: Hunter House.
Kolto-Rivera, M.E. 2004. The psychology of worldviews. *Review of General Psychology* 8, no. 1: 3–58.
Martin, T.L., and K.J. Doka. 2000. *Men don't cry ... women do: Transcending gender stereotypes of grief.* Philadelphia: Bruner Mazel.
MCEETYA (Ministerial Council on Employment, Education, Training and Youth Affairs). 1999. Adelaide Declaration on National Goals for Schooling in the Twenty-First Century. MCEETYA website. http://www.mceetya.edu.au/mceetya/nationalgoals/index.htm (accessed February 2008).

Rowling, L. 1995. Disenfranchised grief of teachers. *Omega: Journal of Death and Dying* 31, no. 4: 317–29.

———. 2000. *MindMatters: A whole school approach to loss and grief.* Canberra, Department of Health and Aged Care. http://www.curriculum.edu.au/mindmatters (accessed February 21, 2008).

———. 2002. Youth and disenfranchised grief. In *Disenfranchised grief: New directions, challenges and strategies for practice,* ed. K.J. Doka. Champaign, IL: Research Press.

———. 2003. *Grief in school communities: Effective support strategies.* Buckingham: Open University Press.

———. 2005. Loss and grief in school communities. In *Brief interventions with bereaved children,* ed. B. Monroe and F. Kraus. Oxford: Oxford University Press.

Rowling, L., and S. Gehrig. 1998. *Mental health of young people: Exploring the relationship between alienation from school, resilience, coping and spiritual health.* Paper presented at Research in Education: Does It Count AARE Conference, Melbourne, Australia. http://www.aare.edu.au/98pap/row98371.htm

Twenge, J. 2000. The age of anxiety: Birth cohort change in anxiety and neuroticism 1952–1993. *Journal of Personality and Social Psychology* 79, no. 6: 1007–21.

Ward, B., and P. Houghton. 1988. *Good grief: Talking and learning about loss and grief.* London: Jessica Kingsley.

Weber, Z., L. Rowling, and L. Scanlon. 2007. It's like … a confronting issue: Life changing narratives of young people. *Qualitative Health Research* 17, no. 7: 945–53.

WHOQOL Group. 1998. World Health Organization quality of life assessment (WHOQOL): development and general psychometric properties. *Social Science and Medicine,* 46: 1569–85.

Living and dying: a window on (Christian) children's spirituality

Elaine Champagne

Introduction

Twenty 10-to-12-year-old children were sitting in a large circular tent. The only furniture in the tent was a long and low bench, close to the wall, with a white cloth folded and set to one side. The children had been invited into Jesus' tomb by two adults dressed as the biblical characters Nicodemus and Joseph of Arimathea. A light smell of perfumed oil and incense filled the space. I was sitting among the children, attentive to what was happening. The children's faces showed expectation and curiosity. Another adult, standing among the children, started the conversation: 'Tell me. Does it happen that you ever think about death?' The reaction was quick as lightning and took me by surprise: hands were up, fingers wriggling, bodies moving, children wanting to talk.

The origin of the experience in the tent traces back to 2004, when in the context of Christian faith education, I was asked by the diocese of Saint-Jean-Longueuil from the province of Québec to develop initiatory sessions for children, which would include their life experiences and be supportive of their spiritual journey. The purpose of the programme, entitled the Grande Halte, was to engage children in an experiential encounter with the Paschal mystery, that is, the death and resurrection of Christ and its proposed meaning for Christians and all human beings. The essence of the approach was to have children as active subjects rather than passive objects. This was especially relevant in terms of their concern about living and dying. Because of this specific dynamic, it was clear from the beginning that the role adults would take in the actual setting of the programme would be specific to this process. With the aid of a flexible framework, they would need to journey with the children and facilitate the free expression and growth of their spiritual experience. In French, they received the name *disciples-accompagnateurs*,[1] which reflects the fact that they are not only walking *with* the children in their faith journey, but they are also disciples, also recipients of the witness of other Christians.

In creating the Grande Halte, I was supported by a small group of lay ministers and diocesan representatives. They would take up the role of disciples-accompagnateurs in the Grande Halte and participate in the formation of others. This committee reacted to the development of the content and offered suggestions. When presented with the idea that children will actually talk about life and death, the disciples-accompagnateurs were hesitant. Would children be able to explore the questions? How would they react? Would parents approve of the process? An American professor of philosophy, Gareth B. Matthews (1994), had already experienced this type of dialogue with children, as well as the parental resistance to the questions on death and dying. As he points out, '[Parents were] shocked because the very idea of discussing death with children strikes them as offensively inappropriate' (89). However, our programme did not arouse negative reactions, either among children or parents.

The programme started gradually in various parishes and at the end of the summer 2007, a specific formation opportunity was offered to the disciples-accompagnateurs, at their request, addressing specifically 'how to talk about death with children'. One of the disciples-accompagnateurs' concerns was a lack of information about children's development in understanding death. But it soon became obvious to all that the main resistance came from the discomfort the subject raised for their own adults' spiritual life and journey. To lead this type of conversation with children, the disciples-accompagnateurs need to be capable of listening to the questions children raise and to deal with the effects on them, so that they can remain focused at what the children are saying and interact with them.

Children's active participation in a communicative model of religious education can contribute to its spiritual development (Dillen 2007). But while faith and beliefs about living and dying can be understood as major constituents of spiritual journeys, they are seldom addressed in conversation with children. Except in crisis situations, parents and religious or spiritual educators seldom listen to children's experience and their reflection on life and death. Yet, this need was long highlighted by children themselves (Darcy-Bérubé 1970).

As a result of my involvement in the creation of the programme, my objectives in this article are twofold. First, I introduce the main characteristics of the Grande Halte and present children's reactions and expressions when they were given the opportunity to talk about living and dying. In the second part, after a very brief overview of the literature on children and death and dying, I highlight certain socio-cultural issues and initiate a theological reflection on the meaning and the worldviews of the children.

Observations

In gathering data, I used a process of natural observation to study three groups of children. I entered into the tent with the children and took notes only after the end of the meeting. In this first part, I will describe the Grande Halte and introduce children's voices.

The political and religious context

Before presenting the Grande Halte, it is necessary to address the social, political and religious context in which it was developed. Education in the Québec province of Canada has undergone an accelerated transformation toward a lay configuration during the last 10 years or so. The confessional status of public elementary and secondary schools was repealed in

June 2000. Religious education programmes in schools – Catholic and Protestant – are being modified into a programme of ethics and religious culture, in order to be more inclusive, both of the broader diversity and of the changing culture of the population. *Pastoral and religious animation* in schools has been officially replaced since 2001 and 2002, by a service called the Spiritual Support and Community Involvement Service.[2]

Parallel to this process, the main Christian church in Québec, the Catholic Church, not only adapted to this changing social context, but was also involved in a revision of its foundational orientations concerning religious education. In a letter written in 2001, Bishop St-Gelais, then president of the Québec Assembly of Catholic Bishops, indicated some questions needing to be deepened. Those questions included the following two:

- How to change from an approach focused on faith transmission to an approach focused on faith proposal?
- How to promote the experience of meeting with Christ rather than solely teaching truths to transmit?[3]

Beyond the shock wave brought about by these transitions, the various teams for formation within dioceses in Québec began to develop various programmes adapted to the specific needs of individuals. While the dioceses and their numerous parishes had, for many years, taken responsibility for sacramental preparation, they now engage in a more global catechetical approach where everyone participates in the human spiritual journey and where Christians are called to witness their hope.[4] The new paradigm reflects a major change in perspective: Christian formation is understood as inscriptive and part of a model of dialogue.

The catechetical context

It is in this context that the diocese of Saint-Jean-Longueuil offers an initiatory programme called the Grande Halte, which follows three years of religious education for children, consistent with this orientation. The Grande Halte consists of a few meetings with children from nine years of age, for a total duration of about six hours. It is perceived as a *relay* on the road, a pause during a pilgrimage or a time of *retreat,* and is part of an intensive period of preparation prior to the celebration of the sacraments of initiation – Baptism, Confirmation and Eucharist.

The approach used in the Grande Halte aims at supporting children's (Christian) spiritual experience. Hence, children are invited to share their experience and to put forth their questions and insights about their life, their values, the challenges they encounter, their hopes and fears, their personal prayer. The approach is inductive and initiatory: children are invited to become part of a story, through biblical narratives and through gestures and the use of symbols suggestive of meanings born by the Paschal mystery and communicated through the Christian tradition.

The Grande Halte considers the children, not only as active subjects, but also partners in the approach. It requires hearing their voices, as well as those of their parents or godparents. All freely participate in the programme. It is an attempt to actualise a Church experience of a shared journey, in an effort to deepen faith in Christ. In its process, the Grande Halte could also be qualified as liturgical, more performative than explanatory.

The participants

Participants in the first Grande Halte included children and parents, the latter sometimes acting as disciples-accompagnateurs or volunteers. They were from a suburban area with a wide variety of ethnic and socioeconomic origins. An estimated 4000 children have entered the programme in the last three years (2004–7), approximately 2000 of these in the year 2006/7. The great majority of children were from 9 to 11 years old. An adapted programme for teenagers is under preparation. All the children had previously participated in a three-year religious formation, but the secular environment in which they lived influenced them considerably. I will return to this point later. Parent or adolescent volunteers gathered and prepared the needed material, dressed up, and featured the different biblical characters that the children would encounter during their *pilgrimage*. Adult disciples-accompagnateurs led groups of 15 to 40 children. Most of these disciples-accompagnateurs were lay ministers, catechists or trainers employed by the diocese. They previously experienced the programme for themselves and received a complementary formation toward it. At least one parent and/ or godparent was invited to participate in the whole programme with each child. On some occasions, they were called upon for a specific contribution.

In the three groups that I witnessed, parents were present and actively participated while also allowing all the space necessary for their child. Approximately a third of these were men. Some mentioned how their child was appreciative of the meetings, singing the theme song everywhere all day long. Among themselves, parents talked about their many commitments, while it was clear that they had chosen to be there and showed no resistance. They also talked with enthusiasm about the coming sacramental celebration.

The course of the programme

It is not the purpose of this article to describe at length the course of the programme. A document in use in the diocese is expected to be published in the near future, after a few years of experimentation. The programme is still under revision. However, a brief overview may be useful in order to perceive more clearly the context in which the children shared their experience and reflection.

The Grande Halte includes four phases. In the first one, the children, after having answered the invitation to join in a pilgrimage toward the celebration of the sacraments of initiation, receive a pilgrim's staff, handcrafted by their parents. On the road, they encounter three characters with whom they dialogue, reflecting about the stories of 'the good things they enjoy in their lives' with the baker, the stories of 'the hard times they experienced and how they were helped out' with the person helped by the Samaritan, and the stories about 'the situations where they took care or took charge with benevolent attitudes toward others' with King David. The road leads the children at the bottom of a wooden cross without body. There, they share prayer.

On their return for the second phase, the group meets with Nicodemus and Joseph of Arimathea. Both men tell the story of what they did at Jesus' death and the sorrow of their loss. They invite the children to follow them into the tomb where they will bury him. At that point, I once heard a child say 'Cool!' with enthusiasm. The children then walk into the vast tent that has been built in the sanctuary, when possible. The parents stay outside. The children in the tent are asked if they ever thought about death. Following the dialogue, a poetical text is heard, from the Paschal Liturgy. The listeners are invited to follow Jesus, who *went down* to awaken all the ones lying in the shadow of death, Adam and Eve, Abraham, Moses, the prophets, and all the ones that preceded us in faith. 'Wake up and rise! Let us leave this place! The feast is ready!' From the outside of the tent, a voice calls every child by his/her name: 'Jonathan, rise up and come out!' A parent welcomes the child and shows a water basin where both silently make the sign of the cross. All can read, printed on the outside of the tent, 'Buried in death with Christ, with Him we will rise from the dead'.

Through the same type of approach, the third and the fourth phases aim to explore the affirmation of the presence of the Holy Spirit and of Christians' witness of the Resurrection in contemporary daily life.

Children's voices

Let us now focus on children's expression of the experience of death in their lives. The comments I present here come from three different groups which experienced the Grande Halte during the spring of 2007. As mentioned, I used a process of natural observation to study the three groups. I entered into the tent with the children and took notes only after the end of the meeting. I realise the sample of data is small, and I do not claim that it is representative. However I believe that children's comments can reveal significant insights.

Spontaneity

It was already mentioned that the Grande Halte was designed to support children's experience and their expression of it, while presenting them with elements of the Christian faith. A first observation of three such groups points out children's spontaneity and openness to talk about death. In all the groups I have witnessed, children were keen to talk, addressing the disciple-accompagnateur, looking at each other, expressing their sadness, their questions, their hope. There was no heaviness during the conversation, but the children were intent in telling their experiences. The disciple-accompagnateur simply listened to them, mirroring their words, being present and gently supporting the flow of their conversation.

Sharing experiences

The first comments from one group featured the various losses the children had experienced: grandparents, great-grandparents, a dog, a cat. They said they missed them. A child said she missed her teacher, who was away because she was pregnant. Another mentioned he had lost a friend through betrayal. In a second group, similar comments were heard. A child had a friend whose brother had died. Another had heard about an adult neighbour who was dead.

In a third group, the first child who talked mentioned,

- Death. It makes you think about suffering. Sometimes, some people suffer and they prefer to die.
- You are talking about suicide?
- Yeah …

In that group, many children had relatives or people of their acquaintance who had committed suicide. They named the people they knew. A little later, a child said,

- Jesus, on the cross. He had suffered.

Many talked about suffering. They were sad, with a little nervousness in their gestures and speech. But they did not verbalise their questions or worry more precisely. In the first group, when sadness was expressed, one girl associated it with fear and began to talk about paedophiles and what she had heard on the news. Other children did not follow her lead, but two of them rather expressed their own fears.

The second group mentioned many 'small deaths' they experienced on a more daily basis: feeling alone, being sick, having an arm broken. Free association could then be made with the person helped by the Samaritan they had encountered in the previous meeting.

Recognising universality

When expressing their feelings, a child from the second group said,

- It makes me fearful. I don't think too much about it.

Their uneasiness was observable, but not verbalised.

- We resemble them [the ones who are dead], we are a little like them.
- It will happen to all of us.

The realisation that death is universal and irreversible is part of children's normal cognitive development at that age.

Questioning the destination

In the same group, the conversation continued about where people go when they die. Some of the children's comments were that

- Everyone goes to heaven.
- Some must go the hell because Jesus cannot forgive all the time.
- Some people are forgiven, but they do it again.
- You cannot forgive forty times!
- I think that heaven is for everyone.
- There might be a place while you are waiting.
- Heaven is for everyone. Jesus forgives all the time.

Within their hearts

On many occasions in all groups, children alluded to the fact that they talk to the deceased 'in their hearts'. It was a source of comfort for many. One child half seemed to make fun of it when he said with a smirk, 'They [the deceased] are still there "in our hearts"'. While listening to them, I realised that for most of the children, Jesus was no different from anyone else: One can talk to him 'in his/her heart'. The children may or may not have had the experience of talking with a family member or with Jesus within their hearts. Overall, their comments did not reveal any causal association between Christ's resurrection and the Christian belief that the beloved is alive 'in God'. What they expressed sounded more as obvious fact to them: When someone dies, including Jesus, you can talk to that person in your heart.

Interpretation

What can we draw from these observations? Before entering into a theological reflection based on the children's expressions, it is worthwhile to consider the contributions of the social sciences within the social context of Québec.

Literature on children, death and dying

Literature on children and death and dying is abundant and very diversified. Expertise to support dying children and their grieving siblings is well developed in the health-care milieu

(Bluebond-Langner 1978; Sourkes 2002). Children's understanding of death and dying varies according to their development level and life experience. Facilitating the expression of their grief by drawing, playing or occasionally by dialogue contributes to their well-being. However, it is important that we consider children's awareness about death and dying before they confront the situation in their lives. Children's live are already affected with the deaths of pets or elder relatives as well as other losses bearing the weight of their signifi-cance: a blanket, a favourite toy, a pet, a babysitter or a friend, the closeness of a parent, are some examples. But not all adults take seriously children's expressions of loss.

An authentic dialogue, and above all good listening, can support the finding of meaning in children's lives. There is increasing documentation concerning dialogue with children on these issues. 'Children need to learn to mourn and find ways to recover, but the way is not always straight' (Carson 1985, 316). Spiritual support is essential.

Clearly, death is not perceived in the same manner by a toddler and an adolescent: they will not ask the same questions or offer the same meaning. Schonfeld (1993), Busch and Kimble (2001), and Hofer (2004) specify the various concepts involved in children's under-standing of biological death, which evolve according to their cognitive development and their life experience, namely, universality, irreversibility, finality (non-functionality), and causality. How a particular child can express his or her perception of death helps us to iden-tify the major challenge being faced according to their developmental level. While the understanding of biological death is important, the question of its spiritual relevance for children cannot be dismissed.

Matthews, in his book *The Philosophy of Childhood* (1994), dedicated a whole chapter to a focus on childhood and death. His reflection examines two pieces of children's litera-ture on death that are very well-known to them: *Charlotte's web* and *Tuck everlasting*. His contribution focuses on sick children's development toward the understanding of their own death, while using data from other authors. He does not report the children's conversations.

Stories and fairy tales offer significant support for children in their search for meaning. The theorist Ute Carson pointed out that 'children need suggestions in symbolic form which help transform their inner needs and struggles into thought and action in the outside world' (1985: 317). Following Bettelheim, she invited many groups of children to talk about and then make drawings of various fairy tales involving separation or death. Her article illus-trates the use that children make of the many elements of the stories involving attachment, separation and relational reinvestment.

Religious stories can also be supportive of this process. Is it necessary to specify that stories, rather than explanation, bear a significant symbolic power? Symbols and characters with whom one can identify nourish the imagination (Salans, 2004). The children can than reconstruct the story from within, playing with the elements and making sense of them. This process is quite different from the simple affirmation of religious concepts, of which Schonfeld warns: 'Attempts to place religious concepts in concrete terms are usually inef-fective and provide little understanding of both physical realities and spiritual beliefs' (1993, 272).

In 1970, within the context of catechetical renewal, Françoise Darcy-Bérubé (1970) studied concepts and attitudes of Canadian children concerning death and beyond. Her aim was to evaluate the impact of religious formation on the children's capability to face the question of death in a healthy manner. At that time, her work was clearly innovative.

More recently, Marcel Hofer (2004) has written a very practical book *Explique-moi la mort ... Guide pour accompagner l'enfant en famille et en catéchèse*, addressed to parents and catechists. He describes children's cognitive development and affective needs in regard to the question of death. He also develops a useful chapter on diverse religious perspectives on death and related issues. However, his focus is not on children's voices, but rather on adults' supportive practices, which can facilitate children's grief or grappling with the reality of death, thus helping them in making sense of their loss and finding meaning.

Cultural ethos

The fact that children were so keen in discussing this topic confirms the significance and the value of the time taken to listen to them. Death is omnipresent in games and news, along with the more personal experiences discussed above. Children from 9 to 11 years of age are nearing a more reflective period of their growth, beginning to perceive existential questions without yet naming them. This is exemplified in their dialogue about suffering and about forgiveness.

However, the views expressed in their dialogue are largely influenced by a 'cultural ethos' brought about by conversations they might have heard or participated in, but also by media of all kinds: music, the Internet, movies, books (Harry Potter), and the news are some examples. If Québec was a society of Christendom up until the 1950s, it now has the attributes of a lay society. Christianity, along with other religions and philosophies, is but one voice in the discussion. There is no unanimity in the population regarding the relative importance of that voice. The recent Commission on reasonable accommodations for immigrants of diverse cultures and religions, held throughout the province in recent months, convincingly illustrates this reality (see Gouvernement du Québec 2008).

While being aware of this context, I was surprised when I listened to the children, to realise that for some children, *Jesus was not different from the other deceased. We can talk to him in our hearts*. A new belief had emerged from a cultural practice exterior to a Christian religious coherence. That belief, too, was questioned by at least one child in one group. I would like to clarify what seems to be at stake here.

What happens after death?

In an attempt to offer comfort and support to grieving children, it is common practice to tell them that the deceased is 'present in a different manner', that you can talk to him or her 'in your heart'. On the one hand, while the language about heaven and hell has been deleted for decades from children's books and catechisms, they still discuss it and even mention 'a place while you are waiting'. The transmission of tradition is strong. On the other hand, the idea that one can talk to the deceased within the heart is a common belief, but without any contextual framework. It is presented as fact, a certitude that is not questioned; it is a lay person's affirmation. It is presented as a truth without a story.

When children are told Jesus' story, his death and resurrection, when they hear that one can be relating to him 'in one's heart', nothing can be more factual, nothing can be less surprising. 'Jesus is no different from the other deceased'. Within a Christian perspective, children's understanding seems to be upside-down. There is no point in Jesus' resurrection: When someone dies, you can talk to him or her already.

An a-religious worldview

Jean-Claude Guillebaud offers an interesting reflection on the question of faith and belief in our secularised western societies, which could bring some insight to this observation. In the first part of his book *La force de conviction* (2005), he comments that we have come to dramatic societal changes, which have left us deceived about history and sceptical about the future. The vacuum left by massive rejection of faith has made us more vulnerable to gullibility.

New ideas are more easily believed in as facts, taken for granted. They exist like lonely entities, outside stories, outside the symbolisation of experience, outside the shared communal depths of the human quest expressed in religions, which have endured time. The new worldview is thus eclectic and fragile. The request for openness to the unpredictable, as framed by Erricker (2007), which can be associated with faith, whether one is religious or secular (Welte 1984), falls into nothingness if no foundational coherence can be found, when no stories are heard. Worse, the new answers fall into the trap of stopping the quest and halting the journey. Rather than being enhanced, spiritual life is impoverished.

Theological interpretation and Christian spirituality

What can be learned from children's words and expressions which can be both significant theologically and nourishing spiritually? The observation opens up many paths. I will choose three which also bear potential implications in faith education. One concerns children's needs, according to what was heard from them. The second mainly concerns adults involved in 'spiritual' dialogue with children. The third appears to concern all of us. It is both a call and a sign of hope.

Stories and history

The children were spontaneous about sharing on death and dying. They were keen in telling their own stories and experiences, open about expressing their fears, willing to reflect together through free associations: 'Jesus on the cross. He has suffered'. They were mature enough to recognise the universality of death, but also to grapple with the question of justice and mercy in an afterlife. They are familiar and mostly comfortable with the view suggesting that they could talk 'within their hearts' with the deceased.

While this view is reassuring to them, it is not questioned, nor it is unfurled in a story, except possibly their own. It is taken for granted, but also disconnected from any belief about what happens to the person who has died: talking to the person within one's heart doesn't say anything about 'where' that person is, or what has become of him or her. Afterlife still remains a question.

I first thought that children would need to ask the question 'why' it is, that we can talk within our hearts. But I realise their need might be even deeper. Not only do they need stories and symbols to make sense of what they experience, but they also need history: the history of a people who shared experiences, questions and a transforming faith through time. They would benefit from religious (Christian) stories and symbols, from an experiential (inner) point of view.

Here again, Guillebaud, and Hauerwas (1981) before him, denounces the rupture with our past, the rejection of our roots, letting our identity become more and more fragile, while preventing us from projecting ourselves into the future. Time is somehow lost along with our history. Children, like all of us, need to discover that history. The questions 'Where do we come from?' and 'Where are we going?' become inseparable from the history of our living faith. The hermeneutical interpretation of our existential quest is indissociable from its collective and historical path.

Come, follow me

I deeply believe that children are not only active subjects of their lives and faith, but also that they can participate in this collective journey of (spiritual) interpretation, if we allow them to do so. In the Grande Halte, children were first invited to 'come and see', to follow disciples of Jesus. In doing so, the children enter into the story which adults offer to them. Yet, listening to the children brought us into a different universe than the one we expected or even realised: What does it mean, in a secular world, 'talking in one's heart';? And why is that even possible?

Children's worldview prompts us to different perceptions of the world. Children require that we also follow them. Hence, we are called to an authentic dialogue. How is it that talking in one's heart sounds like praying? Is Jesus really different than our grandparents for that matter? Why is it that we believe that Christ has something to do with what happens to us human beings in the afterlife? If our faith is experienced from within the Christian tradition and is formative of our spiritual lives, how will we 'always be ready to give an explanation to anyone who asks [us] for a reason for [our] hope'? (see 1 Peter 3 :15–16). We need to deepen the realisation that in faith education, we share the learning.

A risen community

In the Grande Halte, children are personally called: 'Rise up and come out'. However, their initiatory experience also carries a collective tone. When they come out, a whole community is awaiting them. When formation was given to adult disciples-accompagnateurs, they also spontaneously mentioned this communal dimension of resurrection almost as a shocking insight. 'It is the first time that I realise that I am not alone being promised eternal life. It is not only a personal thing. We are many,' said one of them. Being essentially relational, spiritual life – even more the Christian spiritual life – is also about being part of a people.

But there is more. When we enter the historical journey of interpretation shared by Christ's followers and when we allow ourselves to listen to others, including children, we learn from the questions. When we share the learning, we experience from within, and without knowing it, what it is to be a risen community. We experience what we 'proclaim'. The hermeneutical process supports our spiritual experience of the living 'Word'.

Conclusion

In conclusion, it has been noted how uncommon it is in literature that we hear children's words on living and dying. The choice has been made to hear children's experience on the subject during a Christian formation session focused on the Paschal mystery, allowing for their own insights and input. Children's words have then been reinvested as bait for a theological reflection inclusive of their worldview. I deeply believe in the richness that children can bring to our shared spiritual journey. An open window on children's spirituality can lead us to a deeper perspective on our common experience about what it means to be alive and to be called a 'risen people'.

Acknowledgements

A warm thank you to the team members who contributed to making the Grande Halte possible, especially to Remi Bourdon, who initiated the whole project. Special thanks also go to Margaret C. Kiely, PhD, *professeur émérite* of the University of Montréal.

Notes
1. In view of the specificity of this term, I will use it throughout the text.
2. See Ministère de l'Éducation du Québec (2000).

3. Mgr Raymond St-Gelais (2001). See also Assemblée des évêques du Québec (2004).
4. 'Always be ready to give an explanation to anyone who asks you for a reason for your hope' (1 Peter 3:15).

References

Assemblée des évêques du Québec. 2004. *Jésus Christ, chemin d'humanisation: Orientations pour la formation à la vie chrétienne* [Jesus Christ, the path of humanisation: Guidelines for training in Christian life]. Montréal: Médiaspaul.
Bluebond-Langner, M. 1978. *The private world of dying children.* Princeton, NJ: Princeton University Press.
Busch, T., and C. Kimble. 2001. Grieving children: Are we meeting the challenge? *Pediatric Nursing* 27, no. 4: 414–18.
Carson, U. 1985. Teachable moments occasioned by 'small deaths'. *Issues in Comprehensive Pediatric Nursing* 8, no. 1/6: 315–43.
Darcy-Bérubé, F. 1970. Concepts et attitudes concernant la mort et l'au-delà. Une recherche théorique, exploratoire et expérimentale chez un groupe d'enfants canadiens catholiques [Concepts and attitudes about death and beyond. Theoretical research, exploration and experiment in a group of Catholic Canadian children]. PhD thesis, Religious Studies, University of Ottawa, Ottawa, ON, Canada.
Dillen, A. 2007. Religious participation of children as active subjects: Toward a hermeneutical-communicative model of religious education in families with young children. *International Journal of Children's Spirituality* 12, no. 1: 37–49.
Erricker, C. 2007. Children's spirituality and postmodern faith. *International Journal of Children's Spirituality* 12, no. 1: 51–60.
Gouvernement du Québec. 2008. Commission de consultation sur les practiques d'accomodement reliées aux différences culturelles [Commission consultation on accommodation related to cultural differences]. http://www.accommodements.qc.ca/index-en.html (accessed June 25, 2008).
Guillebaud, J.-C. 2005. *La force de conviction. A quoi pouvons-nous croire?* [The strength of conviction. What can we believe?]. Paris: Seuil.
Hauerwas, S. 1981. *A community of character: Toward a constructive Christian social ethic* Notre Dame, IN: Notre Dame University Press.
Hofer, M. 2004. *Explique-moi la mort ...Guide pour accompagner l'enfant en famille et en catéchèse.* Pédagogie catéchètique 16. Brussels: Lumen Vitae.
Matthews, G. 1994. *The philosophy of childhood.* Cambridge, Harvard University Press.
Ministère de l'Éducation du Québec. 2000. *Responding to the diversity of moral and religious expectations,* Québec: Ministère de l'Éducation du Québec.
Salans, M. 2004. *Storytelling with children in crisis.* London: Jessica Kingsley.
Sourkes, B. 2002. *Armfuls of time: The psychological experience of the child with a life-threatening illness.* Pittsburgh, PA: University of Pittsburgh Press.
Schonfeld, D. 1993. Talking with children about death. *Journal of Pediatric Health Care* 7, no. 6: 269–74.
St-Gelais, R. 2001. La catéchèse: une vision commune. Assemblée des évêques catholiques du Québec website. http//:www.eveques.qc.ca/documents/2001/20011024f.html (accessed December 6, 2007).
Welte, B. 1984. *Qu'est-ce que croire?* [What is believing?]. Héritage et projet 28. Montréal: Fides.

Exploring trauma, loss and healing: spirituality, *Te Whāriki* and early childhood education

Jane Bone

Introduction

The construction of early childhood as unproblematic and a time of innocence is only one version of childhood, a childhood that, as Rinaldi (2006) points out, is a product of cultural and social expectations. In my recent research it became obvious that childhood is a time when a range of experiences are available and far from being cocooned from 'real life', with its mixture of joy and sorrow, young children are active participants in life. At the same time, adults have a commitment to protect children. Children have a right to be safe. In this article, I explore the way that attention to the spiritual can support children in early childhood educational settings who may have experiences of loss or trauma.

The opening statement of the early childhood curriculum in Aotearoa, New Zealand, *Te Whāriki* (Ministry of Education 1996, 9), expresses the hope that children will be 'healthy in mind, body, and spirit'. The whāriki is conceptualised as a woven mat and takes a holistic approach to the child and family in the educational and wider community. Supported by the curriculum document it is clear that the spiritual dimension in Aotearoa is an important aspect of the early educational context. I will combine evidence from research and theory to offer narratives that suggest these perspectives merge in the concept of *everyday spirituality*.

The research

In this article my focus is on the many ways that attention to the spiritual can contribute to the holistic well-being of young children. My research question expressed a wish to find out how the spiritual experiences of young children were supported in three different early childhood educational settings. Three qualitative case studies were set up and I spent time in a Montessori *casa*, a private preschool and a Rudolf Steiner (Waldorf) kindergarten. I was a participant observer with the children, interviewed teachers, and organised focus groups with parents. The teachers were invited to make a video for me that expressed their idea of spirituality, and photographs were taken. This kind of multi-vocal research includes the family and community that surround the child; it is a holistic approach.

Context and curriculum

In the context of Aotearoa, spirituality has specific significance because it is linked to Māori people as *tangata whenua* (people of the land). To be indigenous is to have a spiritual tie to the land, and as Cloher (2004) points out, this passes through ancestors 'whose mana (spiritual power) permeates the land' (47). Because of the damaging effects of colonisation in this context, healing has to happen on many levels, on the wider cultural level and on the personal level, as people from here and elsewhere confront issues of identity and belonging. The early childhood curriculum *Te Whāriki* (Ministry of Education 1996) represents a multiplicity of viewpoints but is presented as a bicultural curriculum and includes Māori and Pākehā (non-Māori) perspectives. The curriculum is holistic, and the whāriki is composed of strands and principles that weave together and include the spiritual dimension; this is particularly obvious in the strand of *mana atua*. Pere (1993) defines *mana atua* as a link between the divine (*atua/ Atua* may be understood differently by different people) and 'the absolute uniqueness of the individual' (14). *Mana atua* refers to well-being and includes the spiritual dimension; it is an inclusive concept that calls on what Reedy (2003) described as the 'divine "specialness"' of every child, which is to be acknowledged in early childhood settings.

Tilly Reedy (2003), an influential Māori woman, had a profound influence on the construction of the early childhood curriculum, a document that 'aims to ensure that children are empowered in every way possible ... nurtured in the knowledge that they are loved and respected; that their physical, mental, spiritual and emotional strength will build *mana*, influence and control' (74). There are understandings in this context that *mana atua* will be actively supported in early childhood settings as a link with spirituality.

A definition of spirituality

Ratcliffe and Nye (2006) recommend using a personal working definition when researching spirituality. The definition I used to guide the research is that spirituality is a means of connecting people to each other, to all living things, to nature and the universe. Spirituality is a way of appreciating the wonder and mystery of everyday life. It alerts me to the possibility for love, happiness, goodness, peace and compassion in the world.

When reflecting on stories of adversity it is obvious that a sense of disconnection is deeply problematic. In her classic study of trauma and recovery Herman (1992) notes that survival has always depended on a sense of connection to others. She points out that in traumatic or threatening situations it is possible to 'overwhelm the ordinary systems of care that give people a sense of control, connection, and meaning' (Herman 1992, 33). Understanding spirituality as a means of connection (Bone 2007), 'interrelatedness' (Myers 1997, 99), a 'we feeling' (Valsiner 2000, 267), and sense of personal harmony (Pere 1993) gives credibility to a spiritual perspective on healing and recovery.

Everyday spirituality

The concept of *everyday spirituality* became an effective way for me to engage with daily activity in each setting, while noting the spiritual. It became obvious early on in the study that spirituality could be experienced everywhere and in everything (Bone et al. 2007). Spirituality is often seen as something outside ordinary existence, so there is a tension in the phrase. The recognition of everyday spirituality acknowledges the long hours that very young children spend in early childhood settings. It also emphasises the practical aspects of spirituality and the spiritual as a component of pedagogical practice. The cultural theories of everyday life (de Certeau 1988) enabled me to attend to the 'treasures of ingenuity' (Giard 1998, xlv) that are accessed in everyday life. They support a theoretical perspective that includes narrative as a means of representing everyday experience as socially constructed and culturally mediated (Dant 2003; Rogoff 2003; Valsiner 2000).

Spirituality, adversity and young children

The spirit may be damaged in a number of ways, and Crawford, Wright and Masten (2006) confirm that suffering and adversity are spiritual concerns. Children may experience distress when they enter an early childhood setting for the first time or when they experience change. These issues of separation or anxiety are something that they can usually cope with, especially when supported by parents and teachers. What becomes harder is when children are experiencing significant neglect or abuse in all its forms (Garbarino et al. 1992). Children may also have suffered traumatic events or accidents that are impossible to predict or control. In these cases resilience must be supported.

Resilience is an ability to survive and adapt in adverse circumstances, and resilience is often thought of as the strength of the individual (Crawford et al. 2006). To see resilience as an individual trait is problematic from other cultural perspectives. In the bicultural context of Aotearoa, it is possible that from a Māori perspective, resilience may be thought of as something that can be supported collectively. Reedy (2003) suggests that *mana* is a concept that can be understood as resilience. She suggests it is important that children are nurtured and become strong in the realisation that 'having *mana* is the enabling and empowering tool to controlling their own destiny' (68). This is an important link to *mana atua* as well-being.

In terms of resilience, the work of Bruce Perry has been influential in understanding the negative effects of neglect and trauma on the developing brain of young children (Perry 1999). His work focuses on the far-reaching neurobiological and emotional effects on children of stress and trauma. From lifelong experience in the same field, Garbarino (2000) suggests that an acceptance of children as 'spiritual beings' (61) would make it possible to think in terms of environments that foster the spirit. He suggests that spirituality may be a 'buffer' for the child and a way of 'bringing worth and value to human experience' (62).

This article proposes that the spiritual may be used to support children who have diverse experiences that include exposure to abuse and trauma. Other interventions may be required and regulations are designed to keep children safe, but the practice of *everyday spirituality* may also be protective, restorative and healing. Paying attention to spirituality when working with young children means, according to Myers (1997), that 'we can learn to care in more open and fluid ways' (34).

Children's experiences

The following three episodes present children's experiences and the environment of the early childhood setting as it supports those children. Peter and Tama's stories are self-explanatory narratives. The final section presents 'fragments' that illustrate different aspects of children's lives, usually in their own words. These narratives resemble 'rhizomes' (Deleuze and Guattari 1987, 22). The use of rhizome as metaphor implies a multiplicity of meanings and underlying connections that are not always obvious from what appears on the surface. The rhizome metaphor is based on its natural existence as an underground system, so that certain flowers or weeds appear randomly in a garden; these flowers are connected by 'superficial underground stems' (Deleuze and Guattari 1987, 22). Metaphorically, the rhizome gives rise to new ideas from narratives that are open to various interpretations. In this article, the following narratives are interpreted through the spiritual lens, and in the discussion that follows it will be argued that acknowledging the spiritual can be a catalyst for protection, recovery and healing.

The kindergarten referred to in Peter and Tama's story is the Steiner (Waldorf) kindergarten. Steiner kindergartens are designed to be beautiful, nurturing, and to be places where the will of the child can be strengthened (Trostli 1998), and this particular kindergarten was no exception. Sylvia and Kristy are the teachers. The narrative fragments as children's voices or notes from the research come from the Montessori *casa,* the private preschool and the Steiner kindergarten.

Peter's story

Peter has had experiences of abuse in his past and as a result his behaviour is troubled, and he can be erratic and disturb the other children. Although he disrupts play and sometimes hits other children, he has a desperate need to be accepted and liked. Peter is very sensitive. His life experiences have almost removed a layer of emotional skin, and so he does not cope well with being challenged or hurt. The kindergarten is a place where he can be supported to practise being with others in a way that is safe and non-threatening.

Sylvia focused on inviting him to help her and says that he is beginning to see this as a privilege and feel important. At the same time, she affirmed his friendships with others, and I heard her agree with him that 'Sally is the voice you listen to, Peter'. Sally is his best friend. Sylvia saw Peter painting and acknowledged his 'good heart'. When he drove a truck through the play of some of the children, she invited him to do some weaving with her. One day he hid on his own in the garden. Sylvia knew where he was, and she simply waited for him to reappear and eased his entry back into the kindergarten.

One day, Sylvia told a story about a boy who had been naughty and whose star was tarnished. However, he did good deeds, and his star began to shine brightly, just like the others. It is a strong story, and I noted that Peter was 'transfixed', as if he was the only person in the room with Sylvia. Over the time I was in the kindergarten (10 weeks), something in Peter changed. I noted that he was being very cooperative and was beginning to find it easier to be close to others. One day he decided to hold my hand on a group outing, he was more confident and referred to himself as 'Superman'. He could negotiate with other children, instead of irritating them and interrupting their play. He was less vulnerable to hurt, and when he was not the 'chosen' one, he was able to cope.

Tama's story

I noticed Tama because he was drifting around the kindergarten; he did not settle and at story time, always lay down on the floor or the bench. He seemed to find it hard to concentrate.

I asked Sylvia what was going on, and she told me he had moved away from the part of the country where he had been living, after his house had burnt down with everything in it. After this traumatic event, his family moved to the city, where I met him for the first time. When his mother left, he sometimes cried silently, and Sylvia would hold him until he was ready to move into the room. He seemed to find it hard to be with the other children and was often on the edge of groups. He sometimes appeared stressed when everyone was inside. Then he was allowed to go outside and calm down for a few minutes and come back with the other children when he was ready.

One evening I went to the Lantern festival. This festival celebrates the change from autumn to winter and takes place at the time of year appropriate for the change of seasons in the southern hemisphere. These festivals in the kindergarten celebrate the cycle of life in a meaningful way, rather than simply being imposed, like Halloween, from different contexts and at inappropriate times of the year. The Lanterns symbolise the carrying of light into the winter months. These ritual events usually involve the whole early childhood community, and Tama's mother had been in and had helped him make a lantern. Along with other parents, she had also been asked to carve patterns into a pumpkin as part of the celebration.

On the night of the festival, we all walked around the lake carrying lanterns and then gathered around a bonfire where there were beautiful carved pumpkins with candles inside, glowing in the dark. The children sang and ate baked potatoes. While we were clearing up Tama's mother returned. She told me that he was already in the car and that he had asked her to come back to collect his pumpkin for him. Afterwards I marvelled about the irony that it was Tama, who had most to fear from fire, who wanted to keep his pumpkin so much.

Fragments

This material is taken directly from notes written during the research process and includes direct transcriptions of children's voices. These fragments from the words of children and my field notes illustrate the use young children make of the imaginative world as they cope with challenges in life.

Sara (I heard Sara and found out later that she experiences conflict at home) –

> Sara is making loud crying noises and holds her arms out dramatically. She is holding the cat and dog. She is telling herself a story quite loudly. Kyra and Moana in the sandpit look at her in amazement but she does not notice.

Carola's dream story –

> The baby is crying all night. It has dreams. It dreams it is in a castle and it can't get away from baddies. The fire brigade have to be called because the baby is in a house that catches fire.

Adam's dreamland (Adam comes up to me, with his hands up to his face like claws) –

> Adam: Sometimes I dream of big cutty, cutty nails, on my cheek, going down my cheek and when I'm asleep nails on my pillow.
> Jane: … all about nails? [I am fairly surprised by this]
> Adam: Yes
> Jane: Where does this dream come from?
> Adam: Dreamland.

Jane: Is it your imagination? If you have a dream you don't like can you switch it off?
Adam: No, it just keeps on and on.

Rosa talks to dolls that symbolise giants (this is part of an ongoing drama) –

Rosa says that if she touches the giants they will not be bad any more. She repeats to herself 'I will change them, I will change them'.

Katie as a dog –

Katie: She's not a wild animal [she is talking about herself].
Other children: She's a dog.
                 I'm terrified of dogs.
Katie: I'm only a puppy; I'm only a baby [they stroke her].

Discussion

In the places where I conducted research, children had a great range of experiences, illustrating that childhood is, as Walkerdine (2004) notes, 'mobile and shifting' (107). It is no longer the same childhood that adults remember; and everyone has a unique experience of childhood. Considered in these terms, the possibility of including the spiritual along with all other aspects of care and education in early childhood education may seem to be a challenge. The concept of *everyday spirituality* enables an approach that sees pedagogy in early childhood settings as 'a practical spiritual activity', in the words of one of the teachers. *Everyday spirituality* recognises the power of everyday actions to change daily life, to transform it into something beyond the ordinary and if necessary to provide consolation for sorrow or loss. It is a way of incorporating spirituality into the early childhood environment without being didactic or intrusive.

   De Certeau (1988) describes the 'strategies' and 'tactics' that inform daily life. He suggests that strategies impose order, and tactics enable them to be circumvented by people who constantly seek to make meaning from the situation they are in. In this sense I propose spirituality as the ultimate 'tactic'. In stories of loss or adversity there may be a sense of being overcome by the 'strategies' imposed by 'powerful people or the violence of things or of an imposed order' (xix). Recovery and healing is possible when certain 'tactics' succeed and there is a sense again of wholeness, empowerment and joy. It is often seen as a weakness of spirituality that it is ephemeral, but in the sense of being a 'tactic' this is its strength. It is an aspect of the tactics that de Certeau (1988) describes as 'maneuvers, polymorphic simulations, joyful discoveries' (xix). It is by use of tactics such as these that transformative environments are constructed.

Transformative spaces

A transformative space is one where change is possible and in the context of events described in this article, is a place offering healing. The following spaces are proposed to be spiritual: spaces where relationships are realised in certain ways and spaces where the potential for transformation is always present as a sense of spiritual withness, spiritual in-betweenness or as the spiritual elsewhere. Again I am accessing the idea of the rhizome because these spaces are literal and metaphorical; they are open and they overlap and can be defined apart from the spiritual or be conceptualised as intertwined with the spiritual. These spaces are themselves always in the process of 'becoming' (Deleuze and Parnet

2002, 3) and are continually changing and merging; they have fluid boundaries. The philosophical approach of Deleuze and Parnet includes an exploration of 'becoming' as a concept that acknowledges the constancy of change. The work of Turner (1982), who introduced the idea of the 'liminal' as a way of transforming space and time, has also been drawn on. The spiritual in-between is conceptualised as a liminal space. A liminal space implies an engagement with ritual that is intended to be transformative, and ritual is a way to bring the spiritual into ordinary life as a transformative event. These approaches support the concept of *everyday spirituality* and cross boundaries, bringing philosophical and anthropological concepts into the context of early childhood education.

Spirituality is reconceptualised as part of everyday life with the tactics and strategies that support it. Mayol (1998) suggests that the tactics of everyday life can be understood through, first, behaviours, and second, by the discourse of meaning that attaches to them. The participants in the narratives already told offer practical examples through their stories as they take up positions 'in the network of social relations' that are part of what Mayol (1998, 9) calls 'the great unknown that is everyday life'. In this sense, *everyday spirituality* can be understood in more depth through the (re)interpretation of incidents and the connection with spiritual witness, spiritual in-betweenness and the spiritual elsewhere – the main themes of the research. In the following interpretation, the narratives that have been shared are related to these spaces, which are transformative in that they provide spiritual opportunities for healing and recovery.

Spiritual withness (Peter's story)

Spiritual withness is the space where self/Other meet. In a pedagogical sense, it is realised through the sensitive teaching that was obvious in the kindergarten. I notice that, although Peter was often impulsive, he was never made the focus of everyone's attention, and this was not a place that exposes or shames children by use of the time-out mat or the naughty chair. Instead of taking this approach, the teachers asked themselves how they might change so that Peter might become more settled. They exemplified what I have call spiritual withness in this reversal of power. Kristy (one of the teachers) told me, 'I avoid the words "no" and "don't", and it's easier now because the people around me do the same; it's really good'. Sylvia, whom I saw most often with Peter, practised spiritual witness by doing everything at Peter's pace. There was no element of force, and she encouraged a sense of what she called 'self-mastery'. She could think with him, be with him, always guiding him, literally and metaphorically, with a light touch. When children have experienced harm, the touch must be the lightest. In his exploration of touch, Derrida (2005) describes the '"spiritual touch" which is *infinite, mutual and immediate*' (182; his italics). Spiritual witness recognises mutuality; it addresses 'the question of being together' (Dahlberg and Moss 2005, 95) and is a form of intersubjectivity. The intersubjective can be understood metaphorically as minds touching one another (Bruner 2006).

Sylvia conveys this sense of touch. She says it is her job to 'make the world whole' for children. She eventually wants them to make their own choices and says that her intention is never to 'cut off their unconscious path to their own destiny'. She respects a child's will. Instead of focusing on changing the child, her spiritual approach is to spend time bringing out the best in children. This is a time-consuming process because a child who has experienced emotional damage can resist closeness for a long time.

Sylvia tells stories, like the one she told that Peter found so absorbing. She designs dances and songs and connects with children through her creativity by making them feel special but never singled out. This is important because even positive attention can cause stress to children. Sylvia's practice of spiritual withness is more subtle than that. She tells me that she has 'a conscious relationship to spirit', and this is manifested in what she does. In her approach to spiritual withness she recognises her 'karmic connections' with children and says 'we are in service to what their needs are and we facilitate that with as much integrity as we can manage'.

Spiritual in-betweenness (Tama's story)

The Steiner kindergarten is designed to be spiritually in-between. The path into the building is winding and scented with lavender and inside it is calm and uncluttered. I had a sense of being in another world when I was there. This is something that is true of many early childhood settings. They are distinctive spaces somewhere between home and school/care and education. As an aspect of spiritual in-betweenness, I propose, early childhood settings can be constructed as liminal space (Turner 1982). They are places of ambiguity, of 'betwixt and between', places where children and adults react with the environment and with each other to create new opportunities for meaning making. The space of spiritual in-betweenness is exciting, full of potential and can be a space that supports healing and recovery.

Early childhood settings have their own rites and rituals. Rituals like the Lantern festival experienced by Tama define the year in the kindergarten. Rituals give shape to the year, and rites shape the day. They make cultural practices visible. When children have suffered an unexpected traumatic event, these patterns give structure to a life that might feel out of control or disjointed. Some predictability is important, and daily rites or more elaborate rituals symbolise stability and may be comforting. As Batten (1995) notes, a ritual 'allows us to leave something behind and to embrace the new, to live in the present moment rather than drag our heels in the past' (24). Perhaps this happened to Tama in the space provided by the Lantern festival. In this festival, light was celebrated, and fire was used to symbolize warmth and vitality. This was the in-between space before winter. In Tama's story, this is important. It was a way of celebrating the life-enhancing properties of something that had been so destructive in his life.

Tama was so often in-between, but when I left the kindergarten he was more often happy and joined in with the other children. He was in an environment that allowed him to be spiritually in-between, that acknowledged this was his time to heal. The liminal space is all about a manipulation of time. Time in the space of the kindergarten was conceptualised differently. It was not a place where children were rushed on to the next phase. The construction of certain rituals supports a sense of the timeless, where time stands still, and the time that symbolises potential for learning and healing is incalculable, the moment before it happens. In Tama's case, the possibility for healing was present. He was actively supported in this spiritually in-between space, and the ritual helped him to move on in his own way and in his own time.

The creation of an environment that supports this space presents ways 'that elude discipline without being outside the field in which it is exercised' (de Certeau 1988, 96). Once a rite or ritual is in place it must be fully entered into by participants, and there the element of control gives way. Space-and-time alters according to the reaction of each person; the spiritual in-between is organised yet unpredictable, a space mediated but dependent on reciprocity. Tama, with the support of his teachers and family, could enter with confidence this space that had a potential for fear (the bonfire, lanterns, candlelit pumpkins). It was not a surprise to Sylvia when Tama's mother told her that the kindergarten was the only school he would attend.

The spiritual elsewhere (children's voices)

The children's voices illustrate my contention that the spiritual elsewhere is a space of 'becoming' (Deleuze and Guattari 1987), a space where children choose to heal themselves by becoming Other. I noted that in this space children are not merely pretending. To pretend implies a conscious suspension of disbelief, and the state of becoming is different. These fragments of dialogue show that children understand that change is always possible. They confront their worst fears and survive; they have power over things much bigger than themselves; they are part of a world where it is possible to be different things at the same time.

In this metamorphic world it is possible to see the healing power of imaginative play. Play is the key to the spiritual elsewhere, and children know that in this space they control their own reality. Children respect each other in the spiritual elsewhere, although adults occasionally intervene. In their play children also show solidarity with the natural world and with animals. The children did not interrupt Sara when she was carrying out her dramatic monologue through the mouthpiece of the cat and dog.

Through the psychological lens, the space of the spiritual elsewhere might be seen as a place of disassociation or displacement, a form of defence (Vaillant 1993). In educational terms 'daydreamers' and people who can slip in and out of the classroom in their minds are sometimes seen as problematic. In spiritual terms the ability to be elsewhere is the ultimate practice of freedom, a 'line of flight' (Deleuze and Parnet 2000, 49) and a form of imaginative play that heals the soul. In young children this ability to play is accepted, and many parents expressed sorrow that easy access to this world of the imagination and creativity was lost in the busyness and stress of adult life (Bone 2007). Through play children remain connected and protected from events that might be hard to deal with. As Paley (1999) notes, in play it is evident, everyday, that children create

> wondrous possibilities of good things happening, just when it may seem that all is lost. If Harry knows that the sun is shining and the puppies are playing, we need not despair. We are safe for another day. (114)

In the magical world of the spiritual elsewhere, a useful adult role is to watch and listen. Children are engaged in their own world, and in this space they relate to each other in new ways and create new worlds for themselves. It is a tactic through which they subvert control and cross the usual boundaries. Sara who was having problems at home could express her feelings through the animals: she was them and not them. By using the animals imaginatively she showed that she knew about conflict. Carola's narrative shows that she knew that things might be bad but that help was at hand and that the fire brigade would rescue the baby. Adam was getting to know his dream world. He knew it was scary, but he would wake up. Rosa was sure that she could change the bad people, the giants. They might be larger, but she was more powerful. Katie found out that she could change from dog, to puppy, to baby in a moment and that by accommodating the fears of others she would receive affection. These were a very few of the incidents I identified as part of the spiritual elsewhere.

The spiritual elsewhere may be a place that all people access when the going gets tough. Adults learn to re-enter the spiritual elsewhere through prayer and meditation, through art or physical activity; children enter effortlessly through imaginative play. They enter a world where change and transformation is a mode of being. In this, they also access their own ability to heal and recover from adversity. They can dream and cope in the spiritual elsewhere. In stories of abuse, the tactics children use to survive are often not acknowledged, but entering the spiritual elsewhere is a means of protection.

Therapeia and healing

The findings from this research suggest that early childhood educational settings are places where the spiritual can emerge as part of everyday pedagogical practice. However, the spaces for connection and transformation described above could also be used in more directly therapeutic situations. Therapy or *therapeia* is from the Greek for healing, and each of the narratives deals with aspects of healing as it relates to spirituality. In times of grief or loss it is possible to feel spiritual withness as a means of salvation. There is strength in knowing that someone else understands, and spiritual withness is a space of empathetic awareness.

The spiritual in-between is a space of waiting, a place that one looks back on, knowing that it was valuable, that it was a healing time. In that space there may be rituals that help recovery, and being in certain environments will be experienced as more helpful than others. People look back to a time 'just before' they had the experience of moving on, 'just before' they felt better or began a new relationship. The spiritual elsewhere is a place where both suffering and joy can be linked. The imagination and dream spaces cannot always be controlled; rather, they are escape routes. If the present is painful, then it can be changed in a moment in the mind. These are powerful therapeutic and transformative spaces that I conceptualise as deeply spiritual.

Conclusion

Caring and effective teachers are always thinking about their approach to pedagogy, and the concept of everyday spirituality that encompasses spiritual withness, spiritual in-betweenness and the spiritual elsewhere simply heightens this awareness. This article contends that in these spaces there is room for healing and for recovery from a range of traumatic events, adversity, abuse and grief. The stories told are respectful of confidentiality because there are boundaries and lines to be drawn when stories are told about real human experiences of pain and loss.

The inclusion of the spiritual in relation to the education of young children does not support a construction of the child as wholly innocent or romantic. The narratives refer to the children's experiences, acknowledge their competence, and also describe special teachers who are sensitive and aware of the spiritual. They are stories of the hope that has to be present if children are to overcome adversity. These narratives support what de Certeau (1988, 125) describes as 'the primary role of story. It opens a legitimate theatre for practical actions'. Practical action, in the pedagogical sense, means supporting all aspects of the curriculum and attending to *mana atua* as an essential part of the holistic curriculum in Aotearoa.

While each case study constituted a specific space in itself, the research process revealed that the themes of spiritual withness, the spiritual in-between and the spiritual elsewhere were evident across each one. These spaces are proposed as a way to reconceptualise spirituality as something that exists in the activity of daily life and not as a wholly inner experience. Such spaces are healing and therapeutic and they sustain the discovery of nurturing and supportive relationships. The concepts of spiritual withness as a form of inter-subjectivity, of spiritual in-betweenness as a liminal state, and the spiritual elsewhere as the place of dreams and imagination, are complex themes that come together as aspects of everyday spirituality. It is hoped that an active recognition of everyday spirituality in early childhood settings will be understood as a way to connect with children who have experienced adversity and for whom attention to the spiritual may be a transforming feature of their early childhood years.

Acknowledgements

I wish to thank all those who participated in this research, children, parents and families. The inspiration you all provided was invaluable. To the children who feature in the narratives (and to those whose stories were not included) – go well and be strong – Kia Kaha!

Note

This project has been reviewed and approved by the Massey University Human Ethics Committee, PN Protocol 02/146. If you have any concerns about the conduct of this research, please contact Professor Sylvia V Rumball, Chair, Massey University Campus Human Ethics Committee: Palmerston North (telephone: 06 350 5249; email: S.V.Rumball@massey.ac.nz).

References

Batten, J. 1995. *Celebrating the southern seasons.* North Shore: Auckland: Tandem.

Bone, J. 2007. Everyday spirituality: Supporting the spiritual experience of young children in three early childhood educational setting. PhD thesis, Massey University, Palmerston North, New Zealand.

Bone, J., J. Cullen, and J. Loveridge. 2007. Everyday spirituality: An aspect of the holistic curriculum in action. *Contemporary Issues in Early Childhood* 8, no. 4: 344–54.

Bruner, J.S. 2006. *In search of pedagogy,* vol. 2 of *The selected works of Jerome S. Bruner.* Abingdon: Routledge.

Cloher, D.U. 2004. A perspective on early Māori relationships with their land. In *Land and place* he whenua, he wāhi: *spiritualities from Aotearoa New Zealand,* ed. H. Bergin and S. Smith, 45–59. Auckland: Accent.

Crawford, E., M.O. Wright, and A.S. Masten. 2006. Resilience and spirituality in youth. In *The handbook of spiritual development in childhood and adolescence,* ed. E.C. Roehlkepartain, P.E. King, L. Wagener, and P.L. Benson, 355–70. Thousand Oaks, CA: Sage.

Dahlberg, G., and P. Moss. 2005. *Ethics and politics in early childhood education.* London: RoutledgeFalmer.

Dant, T. 2003. *Critical social theory.* London: Sage.

de Certeau, M. 1988. *The practice of everyday life.* Berkeley, CA: University of California Press.

de Certeau, M., L. Giard, and P. Mayol. 1998. *The practice of everyday life,* vol. 2: *Living and cooking.* Minneapolis: University of Minnesota Press.

Deleuze, G., and F. Guattari. 1987. *A thousand plateaus: Capitalism and schizophrenia.* Minneapolis, MN: University of Minneapolis Press.

Deleuze, G., and C. Parnet. 2002. *Dialogues II.* London: Continuum.

Derrida, J. 2005. *On touching – Jean-Luc Nancy.* Stanford, CA: Stanford University Press.

Garbarino, J. 2000. Children's rights in the ecology of human development. In *Advocating for children,* ed. A.B. Smith, M. Gollop, K. Marshall, and K. Nairn, 51–65. Dunedin, New Zealand: University of Otago Press.

Garbarino, J., F.M. Stott, and Faculty of the Erikson Institute. 1992. *What children can tell us.* San Francisco: Jossey-Bass.

Giard, L. 1998. Times and places. In *The practice of everday life, vol. 2: Living and cooking,* ed. M. de Giard, and P. Mayol, xxxv-xlv. Minneapolis, MN: University of Minnesota Press.

Herman, J.L. 1992. *Trauma and recovery: From domestic abuse to political terror.* London: Pandora.

Mayol, P. 1998. Living. In *The practice of everyday life,* vol. 2: *Living and cooking,* ed. M. de Certeau, L. Giard, and P. Mayol, 7–129. Minneapolis: University of Minnesota Press.

Ministry of Education. 1996. *Te Whāriki: He whāriki mātauranga mo ngā mokopuna o Aotearoa, early childhood curriculum.* Wellington, New Zealand: Learning Media.

Myers, B.K. 1997. *Young children and spirituality.* London: Routledge.

Paley, V.G. 1999. *The kindness of children.* Cambridge, MA: Harvard University Press.

Pere, R.R. 1993 Taku taha Māori: My Māoriness. In *Te ao mārama 2: He whakaatanga o te ao,* ed. W. Ihimaera, 275–8. Auckland: Reed.

Perry, B. 1999. *Effects of traumatic events on children.* Child Trauma Academy. www.childtrauma. org/ctamaterials/effets_I.asp (accessed February 6, 2008).

Ratcliffe, D., and R. Nye. 2006. Childhood spirituality: Strengthening the research foundation. In *The handbook of spiritual development in childhood and adolescence,* ed. E.C. Roehlkepartain, P. Ebstyne King, L. Wagener, and P.L. Benson, 473–84. Thousand Oaks, CA: Sage.

Reedy, T. 2003. Toku rangatiratanga na te mana-Mātauranga: Knowledge and power set me free. In *Weaving Te Whāriki,* ed. J. Nuttall, 51–79. Wellington, New Zealand: NZCER.

Rinaldi, C. 2006. *In dialogue with Reggio Emilia: Listening, researching and learning.* London: Routledge.

Rogoff, B. 2003. *The cultural nature of human development.* Oxford: Oxford University Press.

Trostli, R. 1998. *Rhythms of learning: Selected lectures by Rudolf Steiner.* Hudson, NY: Anthroposophic Press.

Turner, V.W. 1982. *From ritual to theatre: The human seriousness of play.* New York: PAJ.

Vaillant, G.E. 1993. *The wisdom of the ego.* Cambridge, MA: Harvard University Press.

Valsiner, J. 2000. *Culture and human development.* London: Sage.

Walkerdine, V. 2004. Developmental psychology and the study of childhood. In *An introduction to childhood studies,* ed. M.J. Kehily, 96–108. Maidenhead, UK: Open University Press.

Grief and loss: towards an existential phenomenology of child spirituality

David A. Walters

Introduction

This paper begins with the understanding that there is strong convergence between what may be called 'depth psychotherapy' and the realm of the spiritual. The problem of loss and grief in children is considered, along with the value of generating a corresponding model or phenomenology of child spirituality. Existential philosophy, theology and psychotherapy have a history of looking at human challenge in transformative ways. Such frameworks are examined to flesh out notions of childhood spirituality, particularly with reference to the loss and grieving of 'Simon'. His case is outlined to demonstrate that once the *spiritlessness* of the adult world is confronted, children like Simon may readily take on the pain and suffering of loss. This leads not only to an elaboration of how it is that Simon navigates his existential challenge, but also to a discussion of the value of constructs like *subjectivity, modes of being* and *dialectical movement* in facilitating the healing journey. Hence, the corresponding hermeneutic, that of *the choosing and making of self*, is highlighted as an intimate and valuable part of childhood adjustment to grief. The paper ends with reference to Kierkegaard's belief that children are particularly amenable to existential therapy because of their innate qualities of openness, the desire to understand, and to some degree their possession of innocence and purity.

The grieving child

While it is perhaps difficult to generalise a model or framework of the child's reaction to major loss and grief, it is worth the effort if we are to prove helpful to their adjustment and healing. As experience tells us, children are as diverse as their adult counterparts – each with unique qualities and personalities, each reflecting their own combination of contextual learning and genetic history. At the same time, if one is objective and thoughtful, there are bound to be common themes in what children tell us about their loss and grieving. After all, such is the nature of the challenge that, at some point in time, we all suffer its demands and wonder how to best manoeuvre the learning involved.

In point of fact, Wolfelt (2004, 3) reminds us that 'children in our society are referred to as the forgotten mourners'. Can it be that we have neglected children's needs at such times, failed to acknowledge that the grieving of a child may prove informative to us all? Certainly, to the degree that we can identify *the strengths of children in adversity*, their powers of insight, beliefs, and spirituality, it may be possible to clear a path in the darkness, to join with them in addressing pain and aloneness.

Children often reveal a type of simplicity – an acceptance of, and understanding for, the world – a core innocence if you will, one that makes these qualities difficult to miss. This is not to say that the child is without fault, not prone to strong wants and needs, or susceptible to influences that fail to encourage positivism and resourcefulness. Nevertheless there often remains an overarching quality of goodness, one perhaps difficult to describe, but one that outshines faults, mistakes and shortfalls. Is it possible that this goodness also signals the child's openness to change, a type of spirituality in keeping with each child's particular stage of development? In an effort to address this very issue, Søren Kierkegaard (1813–55), father of existentialism, asks us to reflect on the nature of certain childhood qualities:

> Place a child in a den of thieves, but the child must not remain there so long as it becomes itself perverted, hence let it remain there only a very short time; then let it come home and tell of all its experiences: you will see that the child, who (like every child) is a *good observer and has an excellent memory*, will tell everything with the utmost detail, yet in such a way that in a sense the most important things are omitted, so that one who did not know that the child had been among bandits would least suspect it from the child's narrative. (Kierkegaard 1946d [1847], 311; emphasis added)

While Kierkegaard appears to recognise the child's vulnerability to negative influence and to perversion of character, so too does he underline the child's great powers of observation, memory for detail, his or her ability to distinguish fundamental truth from the less important. Early formative experience is likely to set the stage for later growth, including the adoption or rejection of certain attitudes, encouragement of behaviours or misdeeds, and particular ways of looking at the world and its happenings. Hence, the child's social and relational context is of key importance to the evolution of values and ethics, paving as it does the eventual road to independence of thought, choice, and action.

To whom does the child turn at moments of trial and loss? As every parent knows, the child will unquestioningly seek the comfort and guidance of adult caregivers, in fact, may grieve the loss of some such within their own family circle. Unfortunately, as Kierkegaard will have it, these very supporting adults may somehow come to play out the role of *thieves within the den*. Certainly, current-day therapists of many stripes would argue that the most important influence on how a child reacts to death is the response of those adults around them (Wolfelt 2004). Within the majority of Western cultures, such role provision is further enveloped within a wider death-denying and grief-avoiding dimension.

For these reasons, many children grow up without experiencing the pain of major loss or grief (Wolfelt, 2004); they are meant to be protected from the harshness of the adult world. Ironically then, the child inhabiting the den of death may be hindered by those who would steal away any *conscious* experience of loss. In sparing the child from suffering, from the pain and working through most likely to furnish insight, adjustment, and healing, he or she is subjected to a type of emotional stunting, a myopia that robs rather than assists. While, at heart, the child of good observation and excellent memory may recognise this *avoidance as defence*, nevertheless, he or she may well succumb to adult influence through both obedience and vulnerability.

The question of childhood spirituality

Existential psychotherapist James Bugental (1987, 241) describes the importance of talking to others 'about that which is beyond [our] knowing ... [as] a way of identifying the mystery that resides in the core of each person'. For children raised in homes and schools with explicit notions of God, church and relationship, there are likely to be readily available avenues for religious understandings of loss and for spiritual discussions that assist in grieving. These supports may (or may not) be in keeping with the child's levels of social and cognitive development. Perhaps regardless of whether or not the child possesses an adequate didactic grounding for spiritual understanding, at minimum, the relational belonging that accompanies social structures of church, school and community is likely to provide essential emotional connections. This principle of relatedness serves as an essential counterpart to the individuality and to the interior nature (*subjectivity*) promoted by existential frameworks (Spinelli 2007). As such, Kierkegaard speaks of the *dialectic of spirituality*; others of the duality of self and of being. Existential thinker, Alan Watts (1951), observes that every explicit duality also represents an implicit unity. These notions all speak of the dynamic tension that comes to bind intentional experience, *the movement inward and outward* that may appear disparate or paradoxical, but in fact represents the oneness of spirituality.

It is important to note that in turning to existential psychotherapy as *modus operandi* (or as a way to map out a phenomenology of child spirituality) there is no suggestion of any *innate* pathology in the childhood experience of grief. Rather, there is 'the inexorable convergence of depth psychotherapy and the realm of the spiritual' (Bugental 1987, 197). While matters of knowledge and understanding (including core notions denoted by formal church teaching) arguably form an important part of many human spiritualities, there are also matters of the heart (or moving of the spirit), considered as either adjunct or as fundamental motivator, depending on the believer's particular frame of reference. Perhaps of greatest importance to existential spirituality (and to others as well), are notions of decision, action and faith. Here, Bugental (1987, 241) speaks of *spiritedness*, a form of active directedness which defies those deterministic views of choice and behaviour:

In contrast, the conception that the person is the ultimately active, initiating, or responsible agent, that what the person does is not completely explainable by an antecedent 'cause' (e.g. parental teaching, conditioning, trauma, environmental contingencies) is central to [this] perspective … [hence] affirming the validity of spirit in human life as a subtle but radical postulation.

Bugental's words, for many of us, speak perhaps *most* clearly of that form of spirit or spirituality we see reflected in the children around us. Their ideas of loss and grief, prayer and otherness may well demonstrate the teaching, conditioning and contingencies of the adult world. But more importantly, if we are attuned to individual subtleties, distinctive shadings, and the fine nuance conveyed by child spirituality, these may signal a form of clear, assured and directed *spirit*. As such, given the opportunity and tools of existential analysis, children will relate their experience of grief to personal spirituality in very open and sharing ways. It is those adults around them who may need to see and to hear in new ways, ways marked by acceptance, respect, warmth and understanding (Wolfelt 2004, 7).

The spiritlessness of Simon's world

Kierkegaard, like his predecessor Hegel, portrayed his vocation as *an authorship marked by pedagogy*. As such, his written works provide a 'detailed analysis of various forms of spirit, shapes of consciousness, types of selfhood, or forms of existence' (Taylor 1981, 354). While Kierkegaard views teaching and learning as important to spirituality and its eventual *hope,* ironically enough he also sees spiritlessness as an outcome of that 'dissipation of individual selfhood created by abstract reflection' (365). Even though learning and reflection lead to *necessary* (i.e. spiritual) choices marked by free selfhood, when carried to extremes they can serve as a barrier to decisive action. Hence, Kierkegaard's phenomenology of spirit is one that sees the individual take progressively more responsible steps to authentic being or full spirituality (marked by transition from the aesthetic and ethical modes of being to that of the spiritual). Choosing and pursuing self, spirit, subjectivity – the gravity of such a venture may be seen as requiring adult levels of maturity, understanding and choice. But, in the midst of handling loss and grief, where is the child to pursue these, to find her bearings in what is often a spiritless world? In many or most cases, the child needs the wherewithal to tap their unique spiritual qualities, in particular a spirituality based on more than *mere* understanding. It is in fact when the child demonstrates complications or prolonged grieving that he or she may be fortunate enough to find the guidance necessary to make spiritually informed choices.

The case of Simon

Simon was a somewhat energetic and precocious eight year old, brought to the outpatient counselling clinic by his mother. She complained of Simon's 'absent-minded' nature. To her, he appeared as preoccupied, absent from what had been a more interactive relationship, occasionally talking with himself in an animated (but inaudible) way. Simon's mother had visited his classroom teacher, who described Simon as a sociable, though well-controlled child who did well academically. She had not noticed anything odd or absent-minded in his behaviour, though remembered Simon explaining that his self-talk was in fact 'talking with his dad'. Simon's teacher had been surprised to hear that his father had 'passed into the light' almost a year earlier, when Simon was in the second grade. She stated that he had briefly shared this with her, appearing *not* to be saddened or bothered in any obvious ways.

In their meeting, both Simon's mother and his teacher agreed that they were at a loss as to *how* they might introduce more in-depth discussion of Simon's loss, and feelings about his loss, with him. In fact, apart from his self-talk, both agreed that Simon had perhaps dealt fairly well with his father's sudden death, the result of a workplace accident. Simon's mother had to admit that for all intents and purposes he appeared to be quite well-adjusted. She admitted that her recent feelings of 'being cut off' from him might have more to do with her own emotional loss and feelings of loneliness. Simon's mother also felt afraid to raise the issue of his grief with Simon, lest it upset him or make her own sense of loss more intense.

Simon's counselling sessions were marked by a degree of focus and purpose perhaps unique to a child of his age; he was more than able to sit, reflect, converse and to share with his adult therapist. (Simon had rejected the notion of play therapy, although he did agree to carry out some drawings in his sessions.) Within a period of weeks Simon had related his adjustment to his father's death. It was true that his mourning had not quite resolved, that his self-talk did reflect a felt-reliance on frequent contact with his dad. While, at times, Simon felt frustrated with the lack of response (hence, the sometimes animated nature of his self-talk), he conveyed a sense of certainty that his dad could hear him. This was a notion he had gained while overhearing his aunt talk of 'people passing on', an incident occurring around the time of his dad's funeral. Besides, this seemed like a better form of prayer to Simon; at least he remarked so when he talked of witnessing others pray during church services (these, he occasionally attended with his mother). Simon also reported that 'mom' seemed 'useless' when he raised issues concerning his father. He had witnessed her crying around the time of the death and felt badly, in fact responsible for making things worse for her. Early on Simon had resolved to keep his discussions one-on-one with his dad, it seemed as a way to keep in touch with him, and perhaps as a *less-than-conscious* avenue to sorting through his emotions and experience of loss.

Simon eventually agreed that it might be worth reserving thoughts and talk with his dad to once or twice a day, more as *prayer*, now that he was able to talk more clearly about his emotional sorting through and its relation to prayer. He not only came to clarify the role of prayer and counselling in his life, Simon was also able to ask questions about the afterlife and how these might relate to ideas about death presented on television, by those at school, and by his family. While there were no tears in Simon's sessions, he did convey, at times, a profound sense of loneliness, the felt need to keep his feelings and questions silent. In this and other ways, he was likely to have been taking cues from his mother and other adults around him. Simon did not voice any feelings of being deserted by his father; rather, he felt badly that his dad had suffered before his death and that he was not able to share in the future, i.e. in things that they usually did together.

Towards the end of his sessions, Simon voiced some interest in talking with other kids about what it was like to lose his dad; he had felt his friends at school did not understand what it was like for him. Simon agreed that this might be a matter he could discuss with his mother; perhaps there were kids at the church, or at Sunday school, with whom he could talk. Simon talked little of his mother, apart from what he identified as her need for some counselling. Simon reflected on some of the ways that he felt better because of counselling, including what he saw as an improvement in his prayer life (now distinguished from a less intensely felt need for self-talk), in more positive feelings of hope for his dad, and for improved communications with his mom and peers concerning what he had gone through. Simon volunteered to bring his mom into the next session.

The pain and suffering of grief and loss

Human suffering may be seen at every turn, it characterises each and every life. It is, by definition, a central theme in the thinking and writing of all existentialists (Walters 2007). While existential views promise that suffering is, in fact, the way or the means to personal growth and (if you will) to spiritual development, this is not a simplistic or masochistic philosophy. There are certainly damaging and eroding influences in the experience of suffering, for example, forms of powerlessness and meaninglessness associated with poverty, disease, minority rank or victimisation (Soelle 1975). These may lead to an erosion of hope, self and faith in the perception that personal suffering is to be a natural part of life (Soelle 1975). Just as importantly, however, existentialism argues that suffering possesses another quality or dimension, *that of promise and hope* (May 1989). As such, it serves as a *signal* for choice and action. What is required, the existentialist posits, is the creative and courageous orchestration of personal change. It is perhaps the depth, the intensity and powerfulness of major loss that comes to trigger moments of choice in the griever. In the words of existential psychotherapist, Rollo May (1989, 123):

> A human being will not change his or her personality pattern, when all is said and done, until forced to do so by suffering; advice, persuasion, requests from the outside will effect only a temporary change in the cloak of the personality.

As such, there is likely to be a period of active reflection and self-assessment in the process of meaningful grief.

From an existential viewpoint, grief is restorative to the degree that loss comes to be examined in a relational sense; relative to the person lost, relative to those in one's immediate circle of family and friends, relative to community, but also relative to one's creator and to personal faith. In his own way, despite his youth, Simon was able to traverse relational challenges and, as part of this grieving process, to make decisions and take action regarding who he was and where it was he was heading. Twentieth-century psychoanalyst W.R. Bion conveys *the* challenge of psychoanalysis as dealing with the *vicissitudes of faith* (cited in Eigen 1981, 12), or with

> the struggle not only to know but in some way to be one's true self, to take up the journey with all that one is and may become, and to encounter through oneself the ground of one's being.

By accepting and benefiting from loss, by addressing it in such an eminently existential way as a challenge of (relational) self, Kierkegaard explains that there is a corresponding movement of stages or modes of existence.

Where the *aesthete* might become stagnant with self-pity, neglect his or her duty to recover from grief, in fact lose their way by means of pleasures and diversions (e.g. to avoid matters of death and grieving altogether), Simon's choice to reach out in order to share his burden – in fact, to give of himself in such suffering – suggests progression to what Kierkegaard calls the *religious or spiritual mode* of being. Here, Hegel and Kierkegaard agree that such stages represent different *forms* of spirit, stages that must be travelled if *genuine* individuality or spirituality is to be achieved.

In applying such an analysis to Simon's challenge of grief, it is difficult *not* to raise matters of development in the child. Simon's initial presentation may be seen as one of *silenced dialogue* ('self-talk' to others), a form of 'self-absorption', perhaps a type of grasping or reaching outward (towards dad, towards God?), one that only *whispered* of his grief. Paradoxically, to outsiders, these qualities may be seen in stark contrast to what (on the surface) appeared as Simon's resourcefulness and resilience. When others look deeper, unknown to Simon, he is seen to demonstrate a striking aloneness, a type of insularity that nevertheless conveys independence of thought, or a type of wisdom in the form of *patience and resilience*. The narrator in Kierkegaard's *Fear and trembling* (1946b [1843]), Johannes de Silentio, examines *silence as lack of insight*, an *absence of will*, and even as the *inability to become more conscious*. In Simon's particular manifestation of silence, there may have been a consciousness that dared not admit his ill-preparedness, his felt-inability to handle the loss of his father in more cognitive and emotional terms.

Much as Johannes de Silentio contrasts the choice and experience of aesthetic and religious modes of being in Kierkegaard's narrative, so too does Simon appear to a move on to a qualitatively different *plain of being* in the reflections and actions attached to his existential psychotherapy. Ironically, to his mother, teacher, peers and others, Simon's silence took on a familiar caste: he was still seen as 'sociable', as 'well-adjusted', his suffering and pain largely unrecognized. While, eventually, those closest to Simon acknowledged change in his character (i.e., the change brought on by working through his pain and suffering), what presented most powerfully to them was that of 'withdrawal' or a perceived failure to meet their own (largely adult) needs.

Dialectic movement as adjustment and growth

Jean-Paul Sartre (1957) emphasises the intensely spiritual nature of existential psychotherapy by underlining its primary focus as one where humans are seen 'as a totality' rather than 'as a collection'. Given this view of the need for human attitude, adjustment and behaviour to be integrated, a prevailing goal of existential analysis is that not only of 'deciphering' the 'empirical aspects' of humans and their lives, but also to 'bring out in the open the revelations which each one of them contains and to fix them conceptually' (68). Each individual *totality*, then, is seen as reflecting a fundamental choice that links one with others, with faith, self and spirituality. As we have seen, the *sorting through* of such analysis requires the *conscious* experience of anxiety and pain, appropriate levels of understanding, but *corresponding deeds and actions* as well. As such, existential psychotherapy does not exclude on the basis of childhood status. In fact, Simon's ability to engage in such therapy (attuned to his individual level of development) with relative ease and considerable benefit suggests that his essential core (or *spirit*) possesses the components and conditions necessary for making existential choices.

Despite characterising himself as a 'nonreligious' existentialist, Sartre (1957, 13) conveys a deeply spiritual approach to existentialism by linking human life and human nature with ultimate truth, action, and as such, with *subjectivity*. Sartre's subjectivity *is* the individual both *choosing* and then *making* him or herself (16). Sartre also characterises subjectivity as 'the essential meaning of existentialism' (17), that is,

> When we say that man chooses his own self, we mean that every one of us does likewise; but we also mean by that that in making this choice he also chooses all men. In fact, in creating the man that we want to be, there is not a single one of our acts which does not at the same time create an image of man as we think he out to be. (17).

The 'choosing and making of self', according to Sartre, is a two-part process of relating outwards in a way that mirrors the inward choice (1957, 17).

In itself this 'subjectivism' may also be viewed as a type of *transformational learning*, one where *action* is (yet again) seen as defining character (Walters 2008). As a devout

Christian, Kierkegaard argues for *subjectivity as truth* – not only does it include Sartre's notion of parallel movement inward and outward, it also signifies correspondence between thought and reality, a type of interaction between woman and fellow beings, the relationship between humans and their faith:

> What an extraordinary change takes place when one first learns the rules for the indicative and the subjunctive, when for the first time the fact that everything depends upon how a thing is thought first enters the consciousness, when, in consequence, thought in its absoluteness replaces an apparent reality. (Kierkegaard 1946a [1834–42], 190)

This is, in fact, the transformation that Simon appears to have manoeuvred in developing a newly subjective view of self-talk as prayer.

This change was an apparent outcome of inward reflection, but also of outwardly directed observation, efforts at greater communication, and Simon's ability to share his time and person with others. These manifestations of transformational learning were not so much a result of didactic instruction as they were *an outcome of felt experience*, of feeling his way in existential psychotherapy. Resulting insights led to Simon's relational view of grief, one that served as a *springboard* to character change and to the consciously experienced stage of spiritual being. Hence, Simon's demonstrated *change in directedness* may also be seen in Kierkegaard's terms as 'thought in its absoluteness'. Such change speaks of much more than an assuredness or the movement from unconscious to conscious, that is,

> *Fullness of thought* speaks of the decision and conviction that belong to a new way of being; it involves the translation of thought into action [and/or] some analogous process, for example of thought into a fixed idea, a variable as it were into a constant. (Bion 1963, 17; emphasis added)

This awareness of the value of *making dialectic movement happen*, that is the notion that it is required of transformative self-learning (in fact, of spirit itself) owes its origins not only to the life philosophy or *Lebensphilosophie* of Nietzsche and others (Sherratt 2006) but also to the existential *philosophies* of Heidegger, Kierkegaard and Johannes de Silentio, and the existential *psychotherapy* of practitioners like Rollo May and W.R. Bion.

The hermeneutic value of existential analysis

In a real way, then, Simon's experience of loss and grief in existential psychotherapy is *hermeneutic*, i.e. one that comes to *recapture, recover and reconstruct* his self in relation to loss. Simon's therapist has come to form one of a very few *authentic* social relationships with him, perhaps serving as a transferential surrogate for 'dad' (i.e. the major loss encountered). This entails the building of a special or *therapeutic* relationship with the grieving child. In Simon's case it has been *through* silence, stillness, presence, non-judgment, witnessing and prompting that he has come to re-attach to his father in a new, spiritual way. At the same time, also through the joint efforts of Simon and his therapist, there has been a *co-construction* of Simon's understanding and spirtedness, that is, through an existential or dialectic movement. To the degree that Simon has access to renewed quality in his relationships with mother, family, and friends, these are likely to prove as *ever-more-genuine* supports – ones that may potentially promote his ongoing adjustment to loss (and withdrawal from the den of thieves). In this way Simon's grief will continue to mature, to maintain a new directedness (spirtedness) built upon dialectical notions of self and spirit.

According to Kierkegaard, the child's spirituality *does* evidence a certain innocence or qualitative difference from that of the adult. This is, specifically, his or her lack of familiarity with wrongdoing, that is, with evil per se:

> What is it then which the child omits [from her narrative]? What is it that the child did not discover? It is the evil. And yet the child's description of what it saw and heard is absolutely accurate. What is it then the child lacks? What is it that so frequently makes a child's narration the most profound mockery of its elders? *It is the sense of evil, and that the child lacks the sense of evil, so that the child finds no pleasure in wishing to understand it.* (Kierkegaard 1946d [1847], 311; emphasis added)

As such, the spiritual innocence (if you will, purity) of the child is distinctively different from the (to some degree unavoidable) corruptness of the adult.

According to Kierkegaard, 'innocence is a state sufficient unto itself and does not require perfection in a dialectical movement' (1946c [1846], 252). This notion may, in a way, address the observation that the young child is unable to grasp certain aspects or ways of knowing; it may also explain the presence of degrees of contradiction between levels of cognitive and emotional development and the possession of *wisdom* and the *directedness of spirit*. Such a distinct stage of purity and innocence may, in fact, be present in children somewhat younger than Simon. By school age, perhaps by way of the corruptibility of the adult world around him, it is likely that Simon had already developed certain needs conflicting with a state of pure innocence (e.g. selfishness, moodiness, malice, etc.). Simon certainly experienced major loss in the death of his father, along with the aloneness, anger, and social deprivations that may have increased his vulnerability to corruption. Hence, by the time of his father's passing Simon had already been travelling the road of stages described by Kierkegaard, one where relating to the world dialectically entails constant choice between good and evil.

Moving on from the view of the aesthete, to an intermediary ethical stage (where distinctions are drawn between good and bad), and then to the religious or spiritual mode is, according to Kierkegaard, essentially a movement of *continuing concern with developing spirituality*. Anxiety signifies the growing consciousness of associated *dilemmas of choice*. 'The decision', as Kierkegaard puts it, is essentially one of opting for faith or not. As an *individual* decision, 'with the very first choice of the self' there has already occurred a certain resolution, i.e. 'the wrenching experience of one's essential religious possibility' (1946c [1846], 253). In the crisis of loss and grief experienced by Simon, there is likely to have been that degree of *good observation and excellent memory* necessary to facilitate, without much opposition, a succumbing to adult influence (i.e. to a set of values and patterns of behaviour that effectively engulfed his spirituality). With a new pattern to emulate, that put forward in existential psychotherapy, Simon's abilities of observation and memory – but more so, those of his innocence and purity – have put him in the place of *model or example* to grieving adults around him, those who have not yet come to exercise more *spirited* choices.

Conclusion

It would appear, then, that Simon's particular strength – or his *saving grace* – has been the engagement and choice-making of existential psychotherapy. In handling loss and grief through a dialectical movement of self and spirit, Kierkegaard essentially argues that the child has chosen a relational mode of being, one signalled by anxiety and marked by personal faith. For the adult possessing a good deal of spiritual know-how, one who has partaken of reflection and dialectical process, there is likely to be fine enough attunement to the child's experience of grief that professional psychotherapy remains unnecessary. Nevertheless, what is required is a *therapeutic type of relationship*, one where reflective dialogue, social sharing, and dialectical movement come to assist the child in his or her adjustment and greater spiritual development. When a grieving child lacks such a context, he or she may remain confined to the darkness of the *den of bandits*, that is, under the influence of those who profess to know *the way out*. To the contrary, however, it is often the child who, by way of innocence, purity of heart, and dialectical movement, *best* serves as example and remedy for grief.

Acknowledgements

'Simon' is used as a pseudonym for a young boy attended by the author in psychotherapy many years ago. His memory, *example and remedy* for grief are greatly appreciated.

References

Bion, W. 1963. *Elements of psychoanalysis.* London: Karnac.
Bugental, J. 1987. *The art of the psychotherapist.* New York: W.W. Norton & Co.
Eigen, M. 1981. The area of faith. *International Journal of Psycho-Analysis* 62: 413–33.
Kierkegaard, S. 1946a [1834–42]. *The journals.* In *A Kierkegaard anthology,* ed. R. Bretall, 1–18. Princeton, NJ: Princeton University Press.
———. 1946b [1843]. *Fear and trembling: A dialectical lyric.* In *A Kierkegaard anthology,* ed. R. Bretall, 116–34. Princeton, NJ: Princeton University Press.
———. 1946c [1846]. *Concluding unscientific postscript to the 'philosophical fragments': An existential contribution by Johannes Climacus.* In *A Kierkegaard anthology,* ed. R. Bretall, 190–260. Princeton, NJ: Princeton University Press.
———. 1946d [1847]. *Works of love.* In *A Kierkegaard anthology,* ed. R. Bretall, 281–323. Princeton, NJ: Princeton University Press.
May, R. 1989. *The art of counselling.* New York: Gardner Press.
Sartre, J.-P. 1957. *Existentialism and human emotions.* New York: Philosophical Library.
Sherratt, Y. 2006. *Continental philosophy of social science.* Cambridge: Cambridge University Press.
Soelle, D. 1975. *Suffering.* Trans. R. Kalin. Philadelphia, PA: Fortress.
Spinelli, E. 2007. *Practising existential psychotherapy.* London: Sage.
Taylor, M. 1981. Aesthetic therapy: Hegel and Kierkegaard. In *Kierkegaard's truth: The disclosure of the self,* ed. J.H. Smith, 343–80. New Haven, CT: Yale University Press.
Walters, D. 2007. The suffering of personality: Existential pain and political correctness. *Counselling Psychology Quarterly* 20: 321–4.
———. 2008. Existential being as transformative learning. *Pastoral Care in Education* 26: 111–17.
Watts, A. 1951. *The wisdom of insecurity.* New York: Vintage.
Wolfelt, A.D. 2004. *A child's view of grief.* Fort Collins, CO: Companion.

Spirituality, loss and recovery in children with disabilities

David V. Erickson

Introduction

The child who has undergone a traumatic physical injury has experienced a significant loss with lifelong implications for almost all aspects of functioning. For an adolescent, it may very well be the first confrontation with mortality. Developmentally, the challenges to identity, body image, friendship and independence are severely undermined. Their focus shifts abruptly from the immediate here and now of youth to a future now filled with uncertainty, compounded by physical limitations. The trauma may also have significant spiritual implications. Research findings have indicated that high levels of spirituality in adolescents are associated with fewer high-risk behaviors and more health-promoting behaviours (Stafford 2007). In the same manner, significant relationships between spiritual growth and the adolescent's initiative and responsibility for self-care have been observed (Callaghan 2005). Spirituality has a demonstrated association with improved decision making, lower levels of violence and high-risk behaviour, and a reduced incidence of depression (Miller 2006). Spirituality is being increasingly regarded as important to the rehabilitation process, so that there is a need to study it more rigorously within different treatment populations and age groupings (Johnstone et al. 2007; Uppal 2006).

Spirituality in the context of health care settings has been described in a number of ways. Frankl (1987) defines spirituality as the need to find meaning and purpose in life, while Reed (1992) views it as a source of connectedness or interconnectedness within oneself, with others and the universe. Martsoff and Mickley (1998) acknowledge the difficulty in defining spirituality in that it has different meanings for people, depending on their world-view and philosophy of life.

Surprisingly little is written in the scientific literature about the spiritual dimensions of loss and recovery as it relates to spinal cord injury (SCI) in children. Recent articles I reviewed focus almost exclusively on the experiences of adults with SCI (McColl et al. 2000; Matheis et al. 2006; Faull et al. 2004). Spirituality and disability as it relates to children is most frequently discussed in reference to their caregivers. While there are no doubt many insights that can be applied to the spirituality of the individual child, it seems all the more important to study their unique responses, especially those of adolescents. Losses that injured adults experience may very well have their corollary in the life of the child but within a much different context and set of meanings (Speraw 2006).

The losses associated with SCI can be devastating to the adolescent's physical, emotional and spiritual well-being. The immediate consequences frequently include motor paralysis and loss of sensation below the lesion. Other effects may include loss of bowel and bladder control, difficulty breathing (due to partial paralysis of the diaphragm), decreased control over body temperature, increased likelihood of muscle atrophy, skin breakdown, and chronic pain. In addition to the direct physical damage, the individual frequently experiences extended periods of hospitalisation, difficulty performing self-care routines, lack of privacy, long periods of time away from home, family and friends, and frequent, often prolonged absences from school. Due to an association of spinal cord injuries with motor vehicle accidents, there may also be the loss of family members and peers, further compounding the physical and psychological trauma (Grossenbacher 1985, Betz et al. 2004).

By carefully taking into account the developmental level of the child and adolescent, a framework can be provided for studying the meaning of a disability and its spiritual dimensions. Specific developmental theorists provide insights into children's development which help explore the spiritual dimensions of disability in children. Piaget and Erikson describe development as a series of stages that individuals work through, one built upon the other (Barnes et al. 2000). Jean Piaget's theory of cognitive development (1985), Lawrence Kohlberg's theory of moral development (1981), and Erikson's theory of psychosocial development (1963) were influential in the faith development theory of James Fowler (1995). To Fowler, children progress through a series of stages, becoming increasingly capable of abstract, reflective thought and can take on multiple perspectives. During adolescence the individual's spiritual development expresses conformity when their belief and behaviour is influenced by others in the group. As they develop, adolescents take more individual responsibility for their beliefs and feelings and come to question their conformity.

The following case study is an example of how a young woman in middle adolescence dealt with the aftermath of spinal cord injury. Her story is an important one, as it describes an articulate individual who can discuss her injury, what it has meant to her in terms of her hopes and ambitions and her relationships with significant others. Haiden's story is far from finished, but she courageously allowed me to share her experiences to date. In relating her story she has made some insightful comments that I feel will be of value to health and educational professionals, as well as to parents and families.

Case study

Haiden is a 15-year-old girl who lost both her mother and grandparents in a tragic head on vehicle collision. The accident left her with a permanent SCI (T_{12}, L_1 paraplegia). Prior to her injury she was an elite athlete who excelled in almost every sport in which she participated, and she also maintained an honours standing in high school. She described herself as having close relationships with both her mother and father. Her mother was the one in whom she confided and from whom she sought emotional support. Her father played more of a physical role in her life by driving her to sporting events and ensuring she received training and resources to be successful. She spoke very positively about her grandparents who would regularly pick her up at school and whom she described as being the type of people who not only showed up at Christmas, but who were there for her in every respect.

When asked to comment on her experience and how it had affected her, she was quick to reply that, it is not what happens to you that is the most important thing in life, it is how you respond. In the same way that she viewed life in general as being a challenge she embraced; this one would be no different. She said she did not believe in fate. She felt that everyone has the power to turn the negative into a positive.

Yet she described the entire event surrounding her injury as extremely frightening – not only the trauma of the event and the loss of the people whom she most cared for, but the aftermath of the injury. Haiden refused to see herself as disabled, a term she found repugnant, since it emphasised what she could not do. Before the accident, everything came easily for her; now it was difficult. She felt the need for people who could give her a sense of encouragement and hopefulness. She did not see herself as being confined to a wheelchair in the future. She wanted to approach life as she had done in the past, taking challenges head on, to emphasise what she can do.

Upon entering rehabilitation after an eight-week stay in acute care, she was asked if she would like to see a psychologist for support to help her deal with any adjustment concerns. She was both polite and assertive in declining such services. Her previous experiences with counsellors in acute care had been negative. She and her family had immediately been offered the services of a bereavement counsellor within the first two to three days of her admission. The timing was extremely poor and offered in a way that she felt was completely insensitive to her and her family's needs. In the hospital, contacts with a psychologist were sporadic and poorly planned, often conflicting with her physical care. The psychologist was also male, and Haiden would have preferred a female. She was not opposed to psychological treatment. She had family friends, a married couple, one of whom was a psychiatrist she felt was competent to evaluate her physical needs, since he was also a physician. His wife was a psychologist, someone she perceived was sensitive and caring.

These were people with whom she had a longer term relationship, which seemed important to her. Haiden stated the accident had changed her relationship with her father in a significant way. He had become more of a confidant, meeting and responding to a number of her emotional needs that were once met by her mother. She was spending more time with him and felt she had come to know him much better as a result. While she had always valued her father, she said she would never take this relationship for granted in the future. People who were important to her could be gone in the 'blink of an eye', which underlined the need to live every moment to its fullest. She mentioned how important her grandparents were to her; she obviously respected them and confided that, whenever she left them, she always said she loved them.

Other people were becoming more important to her. Her aunt, who also lost her mother in the accident (Haiden's grandmother) had been through hospitalisation and surgery and was a nurse, which seemed to assure Haiden that she could call on her for advice and advocacy. While always valuing the importance of her relationships with friends, they became even more important to her and her hope of returning to a more normal life once she completed her rehabilitation, since they accepted her unconditionally. When I asked what it was about her friends that helped, she said it was their interest in her, time talking about the normal everyday events of life and things that she was missing out on. They provided her with encouragement and belief in herself. She frequently had friends in a waiting line to spend time with her.

She described the feeling of connectedness with others as also being very important to her. During her hospital stay, she received the most support and sense of connectedness with younger nursing staff, who she felt acknowledged and respected her needs more than the older staff. People closer to her age seemed to fully appreciate how important it was for her to be asked for her opinion and given choices, including the right to say no, and to respect her privacy. She felt some nursing staff imposed their own personal values on her. In one situation, an older staff member informed her that her clothing was overly revealing, a comment she found demeaning and lacking respect. Haiden was appreciative that the charge nurse, upon hearing of the comment, quickly made amends.

Physical contact was important for her. She liked receiving hugs, particularly her father and extended family members. Haiden responded positively to physical touch from female nursing staff whether it was in the course of treatment or in a spontaneous act of affection.

It was important that people followed through on their promises. If a health professional or nurse indicated they would perform a particular procedure, such as performing personal care, administer medication, or arrange for appointments, Haiden expected it to happen without having to give them continual reminders. She felt she benefited from structure and routine, such as knowing when things were about to happen, having events occur at the same time each day, trusting they would occur in a timely manner.

One experience in the children's treatment hospital gave her a particular sense of hopefulness. When she began throwing up food for no apparent reason, many of professional staff, including physicians and nurses, were called to investigate. No one seemed to be coming up with a resolution to her difficulty. It was a female paediatrician, who said that the situation was completely unacceptable and that the proper treatment would be found! She saw the paediatrician as coming in and taking charge, assuming responsibility for her care and looking at her as a whole person who needed nothing short of the best treatment available.

Haiden felt that a number of professional staff did not have an understanding of what it was like to be an adolescent. She felt they had inappropriate age expectations and displayed difficulty identifying with her needs. As an example, she wanted to have a close relative or friend stay with her, especially in the evening and during the night. She pointed out that it is unusual for any adolescent to be put in a situation where they are expected, for the first time in their lives, to live completely on their own, away from family, sleeping at night in a strange situation alongside people they have never met, and spending their waking hours without the people most familiar and closest to them. She wanted to have her father with her as much as possible, since she felt that, together, they cared the most about her treatment. As an example, her father insisted on the follow-through and timely administration of her medication, ensured her personal-care routines were performed competently, and advocated for her personal safety in being transported for visits to physicians and other specialist services.

There were difficulties in the consistency of her care. This was most apparent with nursing shift changes from day to evening and night staff. Agreed-upon methods of care and approaches to treatment varied considerably. She saw nursing staff as playing a key role in setting the day-to-day tone: different personalities made a significant difference in how she dealt with the daily challenges surrounding her rehabilitation.

Haiden found herself becoming more selective with whom she spent her time. She valued the people who could instil hopefulness, those who were empathic to her situation, and those who were good listeners. There were a number of her friends with whom she became personally closer, while others became more distant and less involved. A number of her friends didn't appear to know what to do or say around her. There were others, however, to whom she readily related: her friends and their parents who were involved in competitive skiing, particularly those mothers whom she felt understood her needs. A number of people she had worked with as part of a local music folk festival were also very important to her.

When asked whether she attended church or was part of any faith community, she said no. This had not been part of her upbringing in her immediate home environment. While her grandparents were very involved in their religious community and she respected their values, she felt that going to church or being part of an organised body of believers had little appeal at this stage in her life. She also said this could change in the future.

If she ever were to believe in God, it would not be in a perfect God. She questioned the concept of an all-knowing and all-powerful God, especially one who would allow the destructive use of power. Haiden had not ruled out the existence of God, or that she might one day believe in a supreme power, but she was not prepared to express such a belief at this stage in her life.

She believed that death is not final. Haiden felt the presence of her mother, perceiving that 'she is still around'. She believed in a life after death but not necessarily in heaven. Haiden went on further to explain that, while a person's physical body is no longer present after death, their spirit lives on. One of her biggest sources of hope was to know that the spirits of her mother and grandparents still existed. She admitted feeling a level of discomfort in discussing her spiritual views with individuals outside her family. She rarely, if ever, discussed these spiritual views with her friends or other peers. It was something she saw as highly personal, not something she would likely bring up voluntarily.

Haiden believed that there are situations over which we have no control. As a consequence, we can focus on what we can control. She said that situations are what you make them and can be turned to the positive. To illustrate her personal philosophy, it was only within weeks of her accident that she began to think about becoming re-involved in skiing and taking up the sport of kayaking, as well as continuing on with a number of her previous interests. She was actively supported by her father on all her future plans.

Discussion and implications

It is helpful to look at spirituality as a journey. Every member of the treatment team plays a role in helping an adolescent find a sense of meaning, purpose, connectedness with others and recognise that there are questions that may never be answered or explained. Everyone involved affirms an individual by walking along side and helping them become who they want to be, as they confront new challenges. By examining a process of recovery from SCI we can learn ways of facilitating this journey.

It is important to recognise a primary concept when relating to a child's spiritual needs: on first glance spiritual care may not appear to be overly spiritual (Westbrook and Viney 1982), yet it does have spiritual meaning for them. The following points are suggested from Haiden's narrative. They include my observations from having worked with other adolescents with SCI. Every point has significant spiritual implications in an adolescent's journey on the way towards becoming well.

- Once the individual with a traumatic injury is medically stabilised it is important that there be an open discussion about the nature of the accident or incident with the adolescent and their family, in order for them to feel everyone is being upfront and as honest as possible. Professional staff, specifically physicians and nursing staff, and parents/caregivers all need to be part of this discussion. The focus of the discussion needs to be as factual as possible. There will be many questions that will not have an answer at this time, such as the total degree of recovery that can be expected. It is better to be open about not knowing. This will be a time of ongoing medical assessments in which the nature of the injury is more clearly defined. This is a time of uncertainty and individuals need active support. These types of discussions may need to be repeated several times depending upon the readiness of the adolescent and family, and the degree of stress they are experiencing.

- The adolescent needs to have ready access to those who are most supportive, whether they are immediate or extended family members, peers, or other familiar adults. Parents also need the support of the entire treatment team in dealing with their questions in as direct a manner as possible. They may benefit from having updated information about the injury, possible implications, and how best to assist the adolescent physically and emotionally. This also means responding to the parent's anger, frustration and pain, consistent with providing that affirmation for the adolescent. Encouraging parents to have contact with other parents in a similar situation can be helpful.
- It is important to ensure the adolescent understands the role of individual professionals and how they can be of assistance. On entering an intensive-care unit and during the period of hospitalisation, the adolescent meets many people, often with unfamiliar designations or ones that need to be clarified. The roles of specialised nursing staff, bereavement counsellor, psychologist, chaplain and social worker are ones that may be very open to misinterpretation. If the professional staff clarify their roles and make an effort to communicate at a personal level, it will increase the likelihood that their services will be used more effectively. Informal contacts need to be encouraged. This may involve dropping by the adolescent's room when they are not involved in formal treatment and expressing genuine interest in them as a person. Casual contacts with family members can also be extremely important.
- Priorities for treatment need to be discussed with the adolescent and their family. Physicians and nursing staff play key roles in directing and facilitating these discussions. They are in a unique position to discuss what the key issues appear to be among the many medical, psychological and social-support concerns. These discussions may often take on a spiritual tone, in that they could be deliberating over life-and-death decisions or ones with long-term impact, such as the decision to proceed with extensive surgeries. Due to the complex needs of the adolescent with a SCI, both medically and developmentally, this is a discussion that is of tremendous importance, as it sets the tone for subsequent treatment.
- Sensitivity to issues of timing plays an important part in reaching out to the adolescent. It has been my experience that many psychosocial and spiritual crises occur at a much later date, subsequent to the injury. Crises often occur not only when the adolescent begins to contemplate the longer term future (something they are not used to doing) but during such experiences as riding in motor vehicle for the first time after an accident, returning home for a first weekend pass from the hospital or treatment centre, or going back to school.
- Knowing when to enlist the help of support services can play a significant role with the adolescent. Through the course of treatment the adolescent will likely establish closer connections with some individuals, more than others. In Haiden's situation she connected the most readily with the younger female nursing staff. These individuals

may well be in the best position to alert other team members to important needs that have a sense of urgency to them. Responding to needs as quickly as possible provides another opportunity for affirmation because it communicates that the treatment team is listening and wants to help. While the adolescent has gone through a life-changing event, they can still see the world as essentially benevolent.

- It is important that the adolescent's initial emotions and behaviour not be labelled as deviant or abnormal but affirmed as an appropriate response(s) to extremely stressful and life-threatening events. This is not to imply that their emotions or behaviour may be necessarily easy to manage. It is when they are feeling vulnerable that we can show acceptance by helping them to articulate their feelings and perceptions and providing alternative courses of action. On one occasion I was working with a 12-year-old adolescent who was complaining about her lack of recreation time during the day. I arranged a case conference in which she chaired the conference. She was encouraged to write down her requests in advance in order that she could formally present them to the staff. The nursing and recreational staff agreed to meet with her. Together they engaged in joint problem solving and arrived at ways of finding time for her to have breaks from her therapies. The adolescent felt very positive about the experience and began to demonstrate more responsibility for her own self-care and improved adherence to treatment.
- After a life-changing injury, there is a need to reintroduce structure and predictability. This can include carrying out personal care routines, meetings with professionals, and participating in recreational events. Haiden responded negatively when she perceived inconsistency in nursing care as it related to the administration of her medications and the timing of personal care routines. She also found it frustrating when health professionals either made appointments that they couldn't keep or were late without explanation. Haiden needed to know that her care needs were seen as being important. Predictability, the keeping of promises, and consistency in her care provided her with a feeling of security.
- When dealing with adolescents it is important both to recognize their need for independence as well as to acknowledging that they may not be ready to engage in adult decision making. Openly discussing this with the adolescent can be very helpful in encouraging them to communicate their needs and to feel safe with those around them. Several times, adolescents have initiated this type of discussion with me. On one occasion, a 17-year-old male wanted his mother to be with him in hospital during the initial stages of his recovery. In the same manner, Haiden wanted her father sleeping in her room overnight. This reinforces their sense of connectedness to those who are important to them while recognising their legitimate need for direction and support.
- The adolescent's environment needs to be normalised as much as possible. This might occur initially by having familiar objects, pictures or photographs placed in the hospital room. Resumption of activities with peers and continuing with school work take on added importance. Haiden's father cooked some of her favourite meals and provided her with a cell phone and a laptop computer with wireless Internet.
- The adolescent remains a sexual being despite their accident and physical limitations. Hospital clothing does not enhance their body image. Encouraging them to dress in ways they feel comfortable allows them the same opportunities they had prior to their injury. Informing them of sexual-counselling services available for people with physical challenges can be a way of both acknowledging their sexuality and providing them with a resource to deal with questions they have in a totally confidential manner.

- Hopefulness is an essential part of healing. Having goals to work towards, as well as having individuals who work with the individual in helping realise these goals, is important. Even when goals appear to be extremely unrealistic, individuals around a teenager can help them gain more knowledge about their condition, introduce them to others with similar challenges, and refuse to limit the positive expectations they have about themselves. The inappropriate use of labelling can also work against a sense of hopefulness. In Haiden's case, words such as 'handicap' and 'disability' were demeaning. While her spine had been severely injured, her spirit remained intact.
- The adolescent needs to be encouraged to tell their story. Telling their story to those they feel comfortable and safe with can have profound spiritual significance. By telling their story and sharing their ideas, feelings and needs, they change their own perspectives and change those around them. Narration brings a feeling of strong connectedness with others. The effect this has on the professional helper can be powerful as they are invited to share the reality of the adolescent and also experience a sense of sacredness. Telling their story provides adolescents with an opportunity to give something to others, an act, which in itself, acknowledges their value, significance and uniqueness.
- While the adolescent may not be a part of a faith community or adhere to a particular set of religious values, they still may perceive the presence of a transcendent power. While the adolescent may be in a stage of tentativeness, there often seems to be recognition that there is more to life than what is directly observed or what exists in a purely material sense. In the present case study, Haiden found one of her biggest sources of strength to be feeling the presence of mother and grandparents, even though she knew they were no longer alive. They were present to her in the form of their spirits, which would never die. She saw herself as one day becoming one of these spirits and perhaps being reunited with her mother and grandparents. It is an incomplete picture but one that sustained and inspired her. It seemed it was an unfinished part of her story but one she was prepared to live with for the present.
- The adolescent may need help in accommodating to the changing nature of their relationships with significant others. In Haiden's case, with the loss of her mother, her father assumed the major parenting function. Haiden became emotionally much closer to him. While her father attempted to meet many of her emotional needs from the parenting perspective, both he and Haiden realised he couldn't completely fill the void left by her mother. Partly due to this, she also became closer to her paternal aunt. Relationships with peers changed; some became more emotionally close, while others became more emotionally distant. A health professional can help an adolescent by affirming those relationships that have become stronger as a result of their experience of a life-changing injury.

Conclusion

The rehabilitation of adolescents with SCI includes not only medical stabilisation and assisting the teenager to adapt to changed circumstances, but it requires an awareness of the spiritual implications of the care-giving process. If one adopts the perspective that every care-giving act is a spiritual one, we begin to view the helping process through different lenses. As helpers, it is important to affirm adolescents by acknowledging their uniqueness and accepting their emotional response to their injury as a genuine expression of need, and not due to a pathological process. We can reintroduce a sense of structure and predictability in their lives as we help them move from instability to stability. By engaging them in the process of priority-setting, we both give direction and receive it from the adolescent. We need to clarify who we are and what our role is in the enabling process. It is important to both know the adolescent as an individual and allow them to know us.

Hopefulness is an essential ingredient of rehabilitation. We can help by encouraging the adolescent to discuss their dreams and aspirations and by avoiding the use of language and behaviour which denies them the right to live those dreams. When their hopes and aspirations appear to be on a collision course with the realities of their disability, we can gently provide them with information and encourage their further exploration. Connecting them with others who have travelled a similar journey can often be very helpful. Encouraging adolescents to tell their story can be extremely powerful in helping them to discover themselves and the personal meanings they have attached to their experience. It provides them the opportunity to tell others who they are, what they value as important, and their perception of the world around them. Their challenge is to develop a stable identity where they can become a complete and productive adult, building on their felt experience of loss to be able to contribute and give to others.

Acknowledgements

I wish to thank three individuals for their contribution to this article: Haiden (not her real name) for her time and courage to tell her story, and for giving me permission to tell it; Sandy Smith, MDiv, for her careful review of the manuscript and her helpful suggestions and insights; and Julie Erickson for her comments and encouragement.

References

Barnes, L., G. Plotnikoff, K. Fox, and S. Pendleton. 2000. Spirituality, religion, and pediatrics: Intersecting worlds of healing. *Pediatrics* 106, no. 4(October suppl.): 899–908.

Betz, R., M. Mulcahey, L. D'Andrea, and D. Clements. 2004. Acute evaluation and management of pediatric spinal cord injury. *Journal of Spinal Cord Medicine* 27(suppl. 1): S11–S5.

Callaghan, D.M. 2005. The influence of spiritual growth on adolescents' initiative and responsibility for self-care. *Pediatric Nursing* 31: 91–97.

Erikson, E. 1963. *Childhood and society,* 2nd ed. New York: W.W. Norton.

Faull, K., M. Hills, G. Cochrane, M. Hunt, C. Mckenzie, and L. Winter. 2004. Investigation of health perspectives of those with physical disabilities: The role of spirituality as a determinant of health. *Disability and Rehabilitation* 26, no. 3: 129–44.

Fowler, J. 1995. *Stages of faith: The psychology of human development and the quest for meaning.* New York: HarperCollins.

Frankl, V. 1987. *Man's search for meaning.* London: Hodder & Stoughton.

Grossenbacher, N.L. 1985. The trauma of spinal cord injury on the adolescent. *Occupational therapy and adolescents with sisability,* ed. F. Cromwell, 79–89. New York, Hawthorn Books.

Johnstone, B., B. Glass, and R. Oliver. 2007. Religion and disability: Clinical, research and training considerations for rehabilitation professionalism. *Disability and Rehabilitation* 29, no. 15: 1153–63.

Kohlberg, L. 1981. *Essays on moral development.* San Francisco: Harper and Row.

McColl, M.A., J. Bickenbach, J. Johnston, S. Nishihama, M. Schumaker, K. Smith, M. Smith, and B. Yealland. 2000. Spiritual issues associated with traumatic-onset disability. *Disability and Rehabilitation* 22, no. 12: 555–64.

Index